CROSSING THE DARIEN GAP

A Daring Journey Through a
Forbidding and Enchanting and
Roadless Jungle That Is the
Only Link by Land
Between North America and South America

Andrew Niall Egan

Crossing the Darien Gap

A Daring Journey Through a
Forbidding and Enchanting and
Roadless Jungle That Is the
Only Link By Land
Between North America and South America

First printing June 2008
This edition updated October 2023
(minor revisions)

Also available as a hardcover, eBook & Kindle

Andrew Niall Egan, Adventura Publishing
www.AdventuraPublishing.com
Email: CrossingTheDarienGap@gmail.com

Library of Congress Control Number: 2008905016

ISBN 978-0-9647940-6-1

Andrew Niall Egan

has explored isolated Canadian forests, endured Central American jungles, and survived African war zones. Born in 1970 in Dublin, Ireland, he grew up in Toronto, Canada. Andrew has diplomas in radio and television broadcasting and print journalism. He has worked as a newspaper features writer, a television reporter and a book publisher. After traveling on a sailboat for a year, he settled in Florida. He is now a real estate broker and manager of a real estate investment company.

About the Cover Photos:

The large background photo is a Central American rainforest in Costa Rica. The back cover shows the author in the Darien Rainforest near the border of Panama and Colombia. (The photos were taken by Andrew Egan except for the photo of the author which was taken by an unknown person with the author's camera.)

If you ever plan to travel between North America and South America, you must consider that there is no road.

Ten hours southeast of the Panama Canal, the Pan-American Highway penetrates the jungle, shrivels into a footpath and dies. The highway resurrects in Colombia, another continent. But the land between the two countries is a vast and primitive realm. On a map the two ends of the highway appear as two slivers of life, separated by the unknown.

Filling this void is a rugged wilderness known as the Darien Rainforest. Because the Darien hinders all contact by land between North America and South America, it has earned the name "Darien Gap."

Yet most travelers never encounter the Darien Gap. When they go to South America they fly or perhaps take a boat. I decided to cross the Darien overland, traversing from Panama to Colombia by foot and riverboat.

I made this decision four months earlier while home in Canada. At that time I was preparing for a three-month journey through Latin America to experience life in the third world and to collect information for a book. Originally, I was intending to travel only from Mexico down to Costa Rica. But, while planning my trip, I read about eight adventurers who had tried to cross from Panama to Colombia overland through the Darien Rainforest. In their excursion only two made it out the other side. Their exploit intrigued me. Besides, I had already planned to visit Colombia — hiking through the jungle would save the airfare.

So I flew from Toronto to Acapulco and began my Latin American journey. I lived in urban slums and mountain war zones as I rambled through central and southern Mexico then on through Guatemala, El Salvador, Honduras and Nicaragua.

Now I'm in Costa Rica. Three months of rugged travel have hardened me for the Darien expedition. Considering the challenge, many doubts cross my mind. Nevertheless, I'm determined to conquer the Darien Gap.

THE JOURNEY BEGINS

At 4:20 a.m. my mini alarm clock shrills. I silence it and sit up. Then I hoist my backpack, stand up, and walk out the door into the starlit Costa Rican night.

San José is asleep. Aside from the hum of the streetlights I hear only my footsteps. I pause to adjust my pack, and I draw a lungful of the tranquil air. It is late March — the end of the dry season. Within weeks the summer rains will burst forth.

A block ahead two figures emerge from a side street, cross the boulevard, then disappear into the darkness. The Swedes — they always hurry. But at least they're on time for our pre-dawn rendezvous.

Like the Swedes, I'm heading for the Tica bus terminal a few blocks away. Before the 1980s the Tica buses traveled throughout Central America. Then revolutions erupted in Guatemala, El Salvador and Nicaragua, forcing the Ticas to relegate their routes to Costa Rica, and down into Panama until peace would prevail. This will be my only run on the Tica line: a 20-hour passage from San José to Panama City, which I reckon will be uneventful.

Yet I've learned to distrust the buses of Latin America. In Honduras, for instance, I noticed the newspaper headlines like "SECOND BUS TRAGEDY THIS WEEK — MECHANICAL PROBLEM SUSPECTED — NUMEROUS DEATHS." In Guatemala, one bus I was riding blew two tires within ten minutes. When we borrowed a spare tire from a passing bus it blew as well.

I recall most vividly, however, one bus journey in northeast Honduras, through the lowlands by the Caribbean. We were motoring full speed down the highway when several passengers noticed a vibration rumbling through the floor. Someone mentioned this to the husky driver, who ground the bus to a halt, then crawled underneath to examine it. After emerging and squeezing into his seat, he bellows, "There's a problem with the wheel. They'll check it in San Pedro." And with that he clunks us into gear and pulls onto the road.

Minutes later a metallic snap jolts our seats. The women shriek; and the men look to heaven and howl, "Please dear Jesus, don't take us now." The driver wrangles the velvet-covered steering wheel — but with no response. We careen down the highway at 60 miles an hour with no steering.

The driver slams the brakes and a squeal rivets the undercarriage. We surge toward the rocky ditch and, a second later, back onto the highway. No steering and now no brakes! Then suddenly the undercarriage plows into the shoulder, and we grind to a halt.

The women fumble out with their chickens. The men follow — now they are swearing instead of praying. Thirty feet from the road, among the palm trees, our front right wheel lies solemnly, spewing a column of smoke. Thirty feet farther the trees give way to a gorge.

Yet I made it through Honduras and eventually into Nicaragua, where I met the Swedes. They told me they were also planning to cross the Darien Gap. Two days ago we inadvertently met once more on a San José

4

street corner. Since we were planning to travel to the Darien at the same time, we decided to travel there together.

*   *   *   *

It is now 4:30 a.m. as I reach the darkened Tica Bus office, obscured on an avenue behind the restaurants and the short, glass office buildings of the downtown boulevard. The Swedes are crouching on the sidewalk, fidgeting with their backpacks. Both are in their early 20s and have been traveling together through Central America for about three months. Peering through the darkness, one of the Swedes glances up and grins. "So you made it!" he greets.

"Of course. Did you think I'd sleep in?"

He chuckles and leans against the wall to wait for the bus. In Swedish his name is Urban, but in Spanish he calls himself Urbano, which, to me, sounds like a Spanish term for a city bus route.

The other is called Matts, in both Swedish and Spanish. He complains often. "There's not even someone in the office," he grumbles. "They had better come soon. We're supposed to leave in 30 minutes."

I ease my pack to the ground. It's laden heavy with oatmeal and sardines — my provisions for the jungle expedition. Soon a dozen others gather. We three are the only gringos (white-skinned foreigners).

After a few minutes someone opens the office door and I amble inside to validate my ticket. As I walk back outside, a bus roars down from the boulevard, sweeps around in front of us and halts by the curb.

To someone like me who has spent much of the last year in isolated mountain villages, the bus seems mammoth. I learn that there are two drivers, with staggered shifts for the 20-hour ride to Panama City. One driver opens the expansive baggage compartments, revealing one compartment for the luggage, and another compartment with a bed inside for the resting driver. The interior is posh (at least compared to Nicaraguan transport). An austere notice proclaims "Only Cigarette Smoking" and the seats actually have assigned numbers.

At 5:10 a.m. a few stragglers board just as the bus roars to life. I recline in my seat. We cruise out of San José and ascend the mountains. By midday we'll hit the Panama border. Tonight I'll be sleeping by the Panama Canal.

The woman beside me soothes her sniffling infant, while my stomach churns as I recall once again that I have no onward ticket to show Panamanian immigration to prove that I will leave their country. But I got into El Salvador — I reckon I can get into Panama.

Tomorrow the Swedes and I will make our way to Yaviza, the last settlement on the Pan-American Highway. From there until Colombia I won't see another road, car or rusty bus — just rivers, footpaths and rainforest — endless, ominous rainforest.

I have some sketchy hiking directions from my Lonely Planet guidebook, and an even sketchier map, dotted with names of native villages I'll encounter on the journey. One village named Paya, in deepest isolation, was once the capital of the vast Kuna kingdom, long before anyone conceived of Colombia.

The trek from the last road in Panama to the first road in Colombia will take several weeks, if conditions are reasonable. I should make it out before "the rains," which transform the trails into mud-traps and the rivers into raging torrents.

A fiery dawn now paints the eastern horizon, illuminating the mist hanging over the mountainside. A small airplane emerges from the haze and soars into the clear sky. The sniffling infant beside me falls asleep. Soon I also close my eyes and slumber.

Meanwhile the mammoth bus rumbles through the mountains, heading south, toward the Darien Rainforest.

PANAMA — AND A TROUBLING MESSAGE

I wake in a panic, my heart racing before I know why I'm frightened — then we swerve back into our lane and the honking subsides.

It's unwise to pass on a blind uphill bend, especially with a bus, and it frightens the occupants. I look back at the Swedes, who also awoke. Matts returns a frustrated expression. Urban just gazes out the window.

The sun shines brightly now as we crest the mountains and descend into docile flatlands. At ten o'clock we turn into a gas station, and the passengers alight to the adjoining cafeteria. Urban kindly gives me a banana. I check our position on my map. "We should reach Panama by noon," I announce. "Two more hours to the border."

Fifteen minutes later the bus driver exits the washroom, wipes his hands in his greasy trousers, and returns to the bus. The passengers hurry after him, lest they be left behind.

I notice another foreigner on the bus, a Canadian like myself. He stayed in the same $5-a-night hostel that I slept at last night. When I pass his seat our eyes connect. But he glances away, offering neither his name nor any acknowledgment that I exist.

The sun rises higher and the road surface worsens. We wind slowly through faded beige hills of dirt. But as afternoon approaches we emerge from the badlands and the road straightens.

Noon arrives, but no Panama. I settle into another slumber only to wake a half hour later as the off-shift driver shuffles up the aisle. "Pasaportes," he demands. "Pasaportes, por favor. Pasaportes, pasaportes." When he reaches my seat, I hand him my passport, which he then scrutinizes with curiosity. The ragged pages bulge with stamps and visas from the half-dozen countries that I've visited in the past few months.

As he continues up the aisle, I examine the distant horizon. A building, which lies stretched across the road, is gradually advancing toward the bus. The building, I conclude, denotes a new frontier — the Republic of Panama.

Within a few minutes we halt by the border checkpoint. The driver encourages us to wait in an adjacent cafeteria while our passports are being processed.

In the cafeteria I order a cheese sandwich. Then I go and stare at a brilliant red parrot perched on a stick by the front door. It offers no conversation so I take a seat by the Swedes.

Our arrival at the border pleases me. I love having my life stuffed into a scruffy knapsack to journey to a lonely outpost, with an untraveled nation before me, and a traveled one to my back. Leaving behind what has become familiar to me in the previous weeks — the currency, the accents, the culture — I stride forth into an unknown land — a land I've traveled only in imagination or through the pages of a dusty National Geographic magazine.

Unfortunately, as I'm musing on such wonders while chewing my cheese sandwich, an obtrusive European emerges. "Are there two Swedes among you?" he inquires urgently.

"Yes," answers Urban, "we are Swedish."

"Well listen," says the tall, bearded man, now crouching beside the table. "I have a message from Paul."

Paul is a professor from England and a wanderer. He has journeyed through more than 60 countries and even climbed Kenya's Mount Kilimanjaro. I thought nothing of Paul one way or another when I encountered him sitting by the road at the Nicaraguan-Honduran border in early March — except that he speaks miserable Spanish and was in a rush to travel through as many countries as possible on his way to South America. A solo traveler like me, Paul also claimed he was planning to challenge the Darien Gap, but I thought nothing of it at the time. Many travelers boast such plans, only to change their minds once they fathom the challenge of the Gap.

I had forgotten about Paul. But now, as this heavily-accented European crouches by our table, I remember him. "Listen," continues the croucher. "You must watch yourselves in Panama City."

"Why?" I ask.

"It's a very bad place," he continues. "Very dangerous — full of muggers. I was talking to Paul just yesterday. In one day three different muggers attacked him. It's very dangerous in Panama City, especially in the Old City. Paul said he couldn't even go to the cinema across the square from his hotel. One American with Paul was so frightened that he wouldn't leave his hostel. Finally, after 16 hours, he went outside to a restaurant next door. Four guys jumped him and stole everything he had. Paul was standing right there. He couldn't do a thing. He said he's never encountered such a perilous place."

We sit silently, pondering the message.

The European withdraws a ragged scrap of paper. "Here is a note from Paul. He says to go to this hotel — it is safe." Then he stands and hoists his pack. "I have to leave," he concludes, and he walks off to a bus traveling north into Costa Rica.

Meanwhile we sit pensively, conjuring images of a sordid city where gangs of muggers stab hapless gringos. Our prospects seem poor: not only do we arrive at a bus station in Panama City's dangerous "red zone" — we do so, according to our ticket stubs, at the ominous hour of midnight.

"We'll have to fight them!" I proclaim. "There's no other way!"

The Swedes stare at me in unison, saying nothing. Then they trumpet their approval. "You're right — we have only one choice."

Delighted with their agreement, I begin scheming. "Okay. Let's get our knives out so we're ready for our arrival in Panama City. If we're attacked we won't be able to run — not with our backpacks. We either fight or we lose everything."

As we discuss our tactics, the bus driver emerges and tells us the passports have been processed. We walk across the road to the immigration building. I meet a Frenchman in the line. I also see the Canadian from the hostel I stayed in last night.

Once more my gut is churning. To enter Panama you need a visa and sufficient funds for your visit. But, like many countries, Panama also requires an onward ticket to demonstrate that you don't plan to remain in the country illegally. I have the visa and the dollars. But I have no onward ticket because I'll be exiting the country by foot through the jungle. The Swedes and the two other gringos have airline Miscellaneous Charges Orders. An MCO can be applied toward an airline ticket purchase, so immigration inspectors usually accept them as onward tickets.

The Swedes pass the inspection. I approach the gnarly-faced officer at the immigration counter. "Visa!" he demands. I show him my visa. "Tíquet!" he continues.

Instead of presenting a ticket I breathe deeply and submit my explanation. "I don't have a ticket because I'm not going to fly out of Panama; I'm going to walk through the jungle from Panama to Colombia through Darien."

Through mirrored sunglasses the officer scrutinizes me as he considers judgment. I stand before him yearning for mercy. "Dólares!" he demands.

"Yes," I reply, reaching into my money belt. "I have many dollars." He examines my wad, pauses, then returns it to me and stamps my passport. I made it.

Now that we've passed immigration, Matts and I wander to find somewhere to exchange a traveler's check. Shops line the road, straddling both sides of the border. After strolling up the street and entering a store we discover that we've inadvertently walked across the frontier into Panama! Then we notice that, aside from us, throngs of pedestrians are crossing the border unhindered — there's even a Costa Rican police officer shopping across the street. Nevertheless I exchange my check quickly and we return to the immigration building, hoping we don't get in trouble for accidentally entering the country prematurely. To our relief, nobody noticed our departure.

This border incident reminds of my border crossing from Honduras to Nicaragua during the socialist Sandinista era, another time I didn't know what country I was in. On the way to that border I met a philosophy graduate from England and we decided to travel together into Nicaragua. After clearing a series of checkpoints on the Honduran side, a soldier motioned us toward another checkpoint. By this time the numerous checkpoints had bewildered us. As this next soldier analyzed our documents, we just gazed around wondering which country we were standing in, until I noticed a government slogan on the wall of the building beside us that said "Death to imperialism" and I said, "I think we're in Nicaragua."

*   *   *   *

Most of the Tica bus passengers have cleared immigration now, so we proceed to customs. With my immigration anxiety relieved, I'm jovial as we empty our belongings on the outdoor table for inspection. Urban opens his backpack and spills a cargo of sardines. "He's a hungry man," I remark to the astonished inspector.

We return to the bus. Within minutes the mammoth roars to life. After easing past the border gate, we gradually accelerate to the familiar drone. Eventually the sun dwindles. Long twilight shadows divide the pastures. We rumble confidently along the winding strand of asphalt.

The five of us gringos are among the few Central American travelers that roam as far south as Panama. But the Frenchman and the Canadian are going only to Panama City where they'll buy cheap flights home. Almost no traveler ventures beyond the cosmopolitan capital into the luxuriant southern jungles that blanket half the nation. Yet the Swedes and I will stay in Panama City only for tonight. In the morning we begin probing deep into the sparsely-populated rainforest along the last stretch of the Pan-American Highway.

Ten hours south of the canal, the highway expires —
and our jungle expedition begins.

*   *   *   *

A warm evening descends over the countryside.
The last splinter of sunlight recedes behind the hills.
Golden lights from ranches and towns flicker beyond
the fields. Soon the western sky fades to black. As we
advance deeper into Panama's interior, the towns
disappear. The cattle ranges eventually sprout bushes
and boulders, then the fields vanish, overwhelmed by
jungle.

Toward midnight, however, the jungle will be
interrupted by the Panama Canal and the glow of
Panama City.

THE LIGHTS OF THE CANAL

From my warm, soft seat I gaze through the bus window at the rugged hills smothered in darkness. Occasionally I scribble thoughts in my notebook. By this stage of my expedition I can write in complete darkness without looking at my paper, a skill I acquired from traveling on many buses through many nights. So far in my Latin American journey I've explored six countries. I started in Mexico three months ago, then continued through Guatemala, El Salvador, Honduras, Nicaragua and Costa Rica. Now I'm in Panama, which makes seven.

The first European to sight the coast of this serpent-shaped nation was the Spanish explorer Rodrigo de Bastidas in 1501. But for the first few decades after they discovered the New World, the Europeans knew only the Atlantic Coast — the land beyond remained a mystery.

In 1510 a member of Bastidas' crew named Vasco Núñez de Balboa settled among a small camp of Spaniards on Panama's Darien coast. Although about 800 other Spaniards had settled in Panama, jungle perils like malaria and yellow fever had killed all but 60. Eventually the settlers appointed Balboa and another man as their leaders. Within a few years the new migrant organized the settlers into the first successful colony on the mainland of the Americas.

To investigate the legends of the natives that an endless ocean lay to the west, Balboa launched a 1000-man expedition into the jungle in 1513. After 25 days of hacking through the Darien, the expeditioners victoriously emerged on the beaches of the Pacific. The exuberant Balboa splashed into the surf, raised the Spanish flag, and claimed the sea and all its shores for his God and his king.

With the discovery of the isthmus, the Spaniards carved trails between the two oceans. Spanish galleons were soon sailing between Panama and newly-discovered Peru. The ships relieved their holds on the Pacific Coast, and then mules hauled the cargo along the trails for 50 miles to galleons anchored in the Caribbean.

During the next few hundred years, Panama prospered into a continental trading hub for gold, sugar and slaves. After Latin America's ferocious wars for independence, however, Panama became an isolated province of Colombia.

As far back as the 1520s, Spain had surveyed the isthmus to consider building a canal. The surveys ceased by mid-century because King Philip II concluded that if God had wanted a canal across the isthmus He would have created one. Three hundred years later the California Gold Rush renewed interest for a quick trans-oceanic passage, so in the mid-1800s a railway was built across the isthmus. The first attempt to build a canal across Panama was by the French in the late 1800s, but within 12 years the project went bankrupt and they abandoned construction.

In the early 1900s the United States helped orchestrate a Panamanian revolution against Colombia. The Americans aided the revolutionaries in exchange for territorial rights to a proposed "canal zone." In 1903 the province of Panama seceded from Colombia and established itself as an independent nation. Within days the new government granted the United States virtual sovereignty over the proposed canal zone.

For the next ten years, American bosses goaded canal workers through savage jungle teeming with malarial mosquitoes. And in 1914 the dreams of the European explorers finally transpired when a vessel sailed from the Atlantic to the Pacific through the completed Panama Canal. In physical terms, the canal divided Panama but united the world.

Humans accepted the challenge to bridge the Atlantic and Pacific, and prevailed. But humans still haven't accepted the challenge to bridge North America and South America by road through the torturous three million acres of the Darien Gap.

The Darien Gap earned its name because it blocks all contact by land between North America and South America. For the approximately 17,000 miles of the Pan-American Highway system stretching from Alaska in the Arctic to Tierra del Fuego in the near-Antarctic, the Darien is the only section without a road.

So far the Darien has repelled every invasion of the white man. The ruthless rainforest decimated the first Spanish settlers in the 1500s. The Conquistadors avoided the Darien, establishing only a few riverside military outposts and a gold mine. In 1698 a colony of Scots settled in Darien. By the next year they had succumbed to malaria and yellow fever.

Today several hundred Afro-Panamanians inhabit Darien's outlying villages. A few hundred natives dwell in the interior. These days the natives worry little about intrusions of modern civilization: the Darien is so inhospitable it repels intruders. In fact the natives call their rainforest "The Stopper." To this day no railway or significant road has ever infiltrated "the Gap."

Nevertheless several expeditions have attempted to cross the Gap by vehicle. In 1961 Chevrolet tried to drive a Corvair across the Darien for an advertising promotion. In the end, hired natives practically carried the car through the dense bush. Halfway through the journey, the summer rains arrived and terminated the expedition.

Despite the failure of the Chevy exploit, the British Army launched an expedition in 1972 to drive two Range Rover jeeps across the Gap. Their venture comprised 60 participants, mainly British soldiers. It included a Panama City headquarters, a rear base, several support bases, a reconnaissance team, an engineering team, a scientific team, helicopter support and frequent resupply drops by parachute. Plagued by endless mishaps, the expedition hacked through the bush foot by foot. After three months the Range Rovers finally emerged on the southern edge of the Darien. The expedition members straggled behind, limping, hollow-faced and covered with sores.

If anything, the British expedition demonstrated the jungle's dominance over man and his machines. Although the British Army did coax the vehicles across the Darien, many expedition members barely escaped with their lives. During the conquest, expedition leader Major John Blashford-Snell remarked, "Now I can see why the ill-fated Scots colony in Darien perished in 1699."

Indeed one member of the Pan-American Highway project died of what physicians described as a mysterious and medically indefinable "Darien Disease." According to one adventurer named Danny Liska, who traversed the Darien in 1961, "There are many people who claim to have made it through the Darien, but most of them are liars."

Information about the Darien Rainforest is scarce, even in Panama. Apparently there are few maps of the region, and the maps that do exist are full of errors. The Darien Rainforest is almost as far removed from the mind of the Panamanian as from the mind of a New Yorker or Londoner.

Some of the most colorful descriptions of this jungle come from the chronicle of the British Army expedition, The Hundred Days of Darien, written by Russell Braddon. Some of his best narratives describe the hair-raising nights the soldiers spent in the steamy rainforest.

> ...he awoke to see no less than three pairs of eyes glowing at him. Terrified, he hurled his petrol through his mosquito net and on to the embers of the fire. As the fire whooshed and flared, the intruders fled...
>
> ...Jack Ross, more exhausted than ever, spent a fourth sleepless night. He could not get used to the jungle's constant, alien sounds — the thudding on the ground of heavy wooden pods...the harsh, baritone roar of an animal that was recognisably cat, large and hungry. . .

For one Sunday church service in the jungle, expedition leader Major Blashford-Snell recited a prayer composed four hundred years earlier by Sir Francis Drake, whom he described as a well-known Englishman who visited the region. Then he added that "I hope his prayer works for us — he died here."

Bulging with jagged mountains and veined with turbulent rivers, the Darien Rainforest is stunning. Her trees rise to monumental heights. The mighty canopy shelters myriad exotic birds, like splashes of crimson and aqua shimmering in an emerald. Dripping with heat, the Darien throbs with life. Howler monkeys roar like lions, insects drone incessantly and silky black panthers stalk silently. To the south the rainforest gives way to the Great Atrato, a swamp the size of the state of Rhode Island.

Occasional teams of adventurers have crossed the enchanting Darien since the British expedition. But for the most part the Darien remains the domain of its two native tribes, the Kuna and Choco.

* * * *

Outside the bus, the land is still rugged, but the highway is smooth and flat. Matts and Urban lie snoozing. Though the Swedes and I are traveling together to the Darien, we will probably separate within a few days. The Swedes want to traverse the Darien as quickly as possible. I want to travel slowly and experience daily life in the rainforest.

Tomorrow we drive our last stretch to the beginning of the jungle. Since we will start at dawn, I lie back to sleep. A few hours later I open my eyes and see the twinkling lights of the canal and Panama City. My watch reads midnight. I look back at the Swedes. We prepare for our arrival in the Red Zone.

READY TO FIGHT

We rumble down grimy streets that resemble the bad quarters of London. Panama City's lavish financial district lies far across town. Like many cities, Panama's capital has safe sections and dangerous sections. We're scouring the dangerous section — the Old City.

After rounding a corner we halt by the curb. As I exit the bus I recall the warnings of Paul, attacked here three times in one day.

We retrieve our backpacks from the luggage hold. The Frenchman and Canadian decide to join the Swedes and me to find a place to lodge. We have the name of the hotel that Paul recommended, but we don't know where it is.

Across the street, music blasts from a tavern and drunkards cavort with prostitutes. We decide to start walking; this area looks too sleazy to linger in, and we're not keen to meet its night-stalking inhabitants. But if anyone is bold enough to attack us, our knives are ready.

As we recede from the pounding saloon, the avenue becomes quiet. Bright streetlights illuminate the shackled storefronts. The side streets lie in darkness. Our surroundings resemble the apocalyptic setting for the movie "Escape from New York."

As we continue down the road, a battered sedan quietly pulls up alongside us. "What does this guy want?" I mutter.

The car stops and a ragged black man steps out of the driver side. "Hey guys, where ya goin'," he exclaims in perfect English.

The five of us look at each other. We determine he's like an unofficial taxi that will drive us somewhere for a few bucks. We tell him the hotel we're looking for and we pile into the car and drive off.

"A friend of ours says it's pretty rough around here," one of the Swedes mentions to the driver as we sprint down the darkened avenue.

The man shakes his head and grins. "It doesn't matter if you get killed here, man. We all gonna die anyway."

Within a few minutes we arrive at the hotel that Paul recommended. We squeeze out of the cramped car and pay the driver. Then we walk over to the thick wooden door and ring the bell. An elderly woman peers through the peephole. Then she lets us in and leads us up a treacherous stairway as in a horror movie.

After we check in, the friendly woman gives us some cold water and she chats with us about our travels. Like the taxi driver, and many others in Panama City, she speaks English. "So you are friends of Paul," she learns. "Well, I'm glad you have arrived. I have a note he told me to give you."

Paul's note welcomes us to the hotel and informs us that he has already departed for the Gap. We decide to try to meet up with him in the Darien, although he's probably already too far ahead.

After we settle into our rooms I wander in search of the bathroom and discover a rickety balcony at the back of the hotel. Twenty-one hours and 500 miles ago I stood beneath the verdant mountains of San José, Costa Rica, the Switzerland of Latin America. Now I'm in Panama City, the crossroads of the world. As I perch on the balcony, the city's lights envelop me. As I gaze farther, beyond the shadowed alleys and ramshackle villas, I behold the grand Pacific stretched along the horizon and gleaming in the moonlight.

So far everything is progressing according to plan; tonight I'm sleeping by the canal.

DARIEN PROVINCE

Four and a half hours sleep, then we rise and repack our bags. As we say farewell to the proprietor, she admonishes us to be careful. "Yes," we respond, "we've already heard how dangerous these streets are at night."

"No, No, No!" she warns. "Not only at night — you must be careful around here during the day as well."

Outside the hotel, the avenue is baking in the morning heat. The Frenchman and Canadian leave to find a bus to the airport. The Swedes and I find a café. I sit on a stool beside a pair of police officers and order breakfast. This is the first time I've eaten pancakes since Mexico. For the past three months I've dined on beans and rice.

After devouring our meal, we visit a bank to get some cash advances on our credit cards. Banks in Latin America are heavily air-conditioned and this one is wintry cold, and I wonder whether these banks measure their status by the degree of their frigidity.

As I stand in front of the teller, I glimpse my filthy and disheveled image in a mirror. Despite my ragged appearance, my white skin and gringo features provide reliable entry to even the most elite establishments, a benefit not necessarily available to the many Native Americans or Blacks in Latin America who often suffer discrimination.

After receiving our cash and concealing it in our money belts, we search for a currency exchange to buy some Colombian pesos. We need to buy Colombian money now in case we board a bus or buy something soon after we enter Colombia — after all, we're entering Colombia via some trails in the rainforest; we won't find any banks or exchange houses until we enter a town hundreds of miles beyond the Colombian border, but we might need to buy something before we see our first bank.

The currency exchanges that we visit have no pesos left. The Swedes want to get moving. "Forget about the pesos," says Matts. "We'll buy them somehow as soon as we enter Colombia."

Our errands finished, we walk to the bus depot. On the way we pass the presidential palace, draped with elaborate red banners wafting in the tropical breeze.

After wandering along some side streets we find the depot, a gravel parking lot beside the ocean. Eventually we find the bus to Darien Province. (It's actually more like a large, rusty van.) We shove our backpacks onto the roof and tie them beside the drums of spare gasoline. The bus leaves at noon, about an hour from now.

Perhaps forgetting that we'll soon be hiking through a muddy rainforest, Matts and Urban recline on a bench for a shoeshine. I wander to the edge of the parking lot to watch the crashing Pacific. On the southern horizon, a line of ships drifts toward the entrance to the canal.

Some friendly taxi drivers, who are hanging around waiting for a fare, begin chatting with me. They can't comprehend why anyone would want to visit the Darien Rainforest, much less spend half a month hiking through the wilds to Colombia. "As soon as you cross into Colombia, the guerillas will pounce on you with your American faces," warns one man.

Few Panamanians have traveled even to Yaviza, the outpost that marks the end of the Pan-American Highway. Any that have traveled to Yaviza have gone no farther. As far as Panamanians are concerned, everything ends at Yaviza; the land beyond is a cauldron of panthers, serpents and bandits.

*   *   *   *

Thirty minutes before the bus leaves, I suddenly remember that I have to phone a friend of mine in Canada. Before I left for Latin America, my family and friends were worried about the war zones I was planning to travel through. If anything happened to me, nobody back home would know. So they made me promise to phone home on a regular bi-weekly schedule. If I don't phone today, I won't be able to phone until after I get through the Gap, a long time from now. They'll assume that something tragic happened to me.

In the other Central American countries that I've traveled through in the past months, you must go to a central telephone office to make an international call. I tell the Swedes to watch my bags. "I have to make an important phone call."

"But the bus is leaving in half an hour," they urge.

"Don't worry. I'll be back before noon. But if I'm delayed try to hold the bus for me."

I flee the bus depot and flag a taxi. "I want to go to the telephone office. And I'm in a rush." The cabby speeds through the streets. We enter the lofty financial district. After whizzing past the Bank of Bogotá, the Bank of Tokyo, the Bank of Korea, the Bank of America, McDonalds and Burger King, he drops me off at the telephone building.

I dash around the building looking for the office for making an international call. I wonder what the other people on the street think of me — this grimy gringo running around with chaotic hair and with toes beginning to peek through his ragged shoes.

I find nowhere in the building to make an international call, and I can't look anymore; the bus to Darien leaves in ten minutes and my backpack is on the roof. I forget about the phone call, and flag another taxi.

"So are you a missionary?" this cabby inquires as we race back to the depot.

"No, just a traveler."

A few blocks before the bus depot, a traffic jam traps us. I pay the driver and start running along the sidewalk. As I run, my eye suddenly glimpses a man across the road sitting on a chair on the sidewalk, backdropped by a faded yellow stucco wall, and surrounded by a profusion of electric fans with a carpet of tools by his feet. What a photo, I think to myself. I quickly cross the road and withdraw my camera from my daypack. "Sir, may I take your photo, please"

"No."

"Why not?"

"Because no."

What a grump. I feel like snapping a shot anyway then running off, but I respectfully put away the camera and continue sprinting to the bus depot.

When I reach the bus the engine is running and they're preparing to leave.

"Did you make your call?" ask the Swedes.

"No. I couldn't find the place in time."

"Just use the payphone on that wall over there and dial 106 — we just did it to phone Sweden."

I pick up the phone and dial. An operator answers and asks which country I wish to call. Within a few seconds I'm connected to my friend's number in Toronto. I tell him that everything is fine, that I'm traveling to the Darien today, and that I'll phone again when I reach Colombia.

I slam down the phone. As the bus starts to roll, I leap through its open front door. As I sit down, I recall seeing a newspaper headline that I noticed as I was running around looking for the telephone office. It said "3000 Assassinations in Colombia in One Month." The bus chugs out of the depot and begins barreling down the road. The newspaper headline lingers in my mind and I wonder to myself, "What kind of place am I going to?"

*   *   *   *

The luggage on the roof of the bus is wrapped with a tarp to shield it from rain. As we speed down the Pan-American Highway, skirting the Pacific Coast, the tarp flaps in the breeze.

The bus doesn't fit the Swedes. Even with their long legs spread wide, their knees press into the seatbacks. The interior is plastered with cheap wallpaper and tacky stickers — some featuring voluptuous blondes, others featuring the Virgin Mary with baby Jesus. A piece of paper stuck behind the driver's seat lists the 29 stops on this bus route. Yaviza is 29.

The bus pulls into small depots every few minutes and waits for passengers. After two hours we've driven less than 15 miles of our 110-mile trip. But soon we overtake the cluster of settlements around Panama City. Then we leave the coast and veer toward the forested interior. A few minutes later we pass through the city of Chepo and we enter Darien province.

Soon the pavement ends. I realize that the luggage is covered by tarp not to shield it in case of rain, but to protect it from the perpetual dust clouds from the rugged gravel road. I also realize why many of the passengers bought handkerchiefs from vendors at the last bus stop. Billows of dust are whooshing through the windows. The people with handkerchiefs cover their mouths. The rest of us tug our shirts over our faces.

The rugged road probes deeper into the interior. We pass several picturesque blue lakes. Logging trucks occasionally rumble past us in the opposite direction. Rocks leap up and hammer the undercarriage, whapping the layer of silt on the floor. Eight more hours to Yaviza.

Every few minutes I notice clusters of thatched huts alongside the road, their haystack roofs drooping in the late afternoon heat. The families in the huts lean out their windows and wave. Even as far south as this, farmers have slashed the land to plant banana trees. At this time of the year the farmers are burning their harvested fields to fertilize the soil for the next crop. As we pass some areas, immeasurable clouds of smoke clog the horizon.

Matts gives me a Hemingway novel to read. I close my window, but dust relentlessly spurts through a crack at the bottom of the window and gradually veils the pages of Across the River and Into the Trees.

After a few hours, we pull over beside a large hut for a rest break. One big black man steps out of the bus and slaps his neck, producing a cloud of dust. With the bus sitting motionless, the air is still and the sun is scorching. But I'm cheerful: I have bananas to eat, I can wipe my hands on my pants, I can spit wherever I want, nobody cares how dirty I am, and I have a free book to read. A few minutes pass, and we board the bus once more and continue down the road.

*   *   *   *

Toward six o'clock the western sky transforms from blue to raging red. In the dimming light I continue reading the Hemingway novel. The book absorbs me; in my mind I am in Italy after World War I. Reading the book reminds me of my youth. When I was a teenager in school I used to skip recess and stay inside with some library books. At times I became so immersed in what I was reading that I didn't hear people who tried to talk to me. Looking up from the book jars me. I am no longer in rural Italy. I am deep in tropical Darien province, southern Panama.

A red strip now lines the horizon, making silhouettes of the drooping huts. Giant ferns rise from the scrub. In the distance the burning fields glow spooky orange.

Up ahead by the side of the road a suntanned boy is waving at us. Clad only in loincloth, he waves, and waves, and waves, then vanishes behind our swath of dust.

We reach Yaviza in a few hours. Only a few passengers remain.

THE GAP

The gravel road degenerates into a dirt track. We tear along the final miles of the Pan-American Highway through the dark, weaving from side to side to dodge the bigger rocks. Alongside the road a lazy river glistens in the moonlight while winding through tall, rustling grass.

I lean out the window. The warm night air massages my face and tussles my hair. I gaze at the star-studded sky. Never have I seen such a mesmerizing sky: from horizon to horizon myriad galaxies sparkle above the jungle. Speckles of light twinkle from the heights of the universe, descend in shimmering strings and hover a few feet above the treetops.

After a few hours I notice a lone streetlight above a junction in the road. We decelerate and turn onto the small side road to Santa Fé, an isolated town beside an army base. After a few hundred yards I see several houses glowing with electric lights. We pull over beside a shabby saloon. Its walls reverberate with Meringue while twirling disco lights illuminate the dusty floor.

In the middle of the town stands a lone pole impaled in the dirt and attached to a telephone booth. The Swedes and I stare at this solitary telephone booth nestled in this remote jungle outpost surrounded by moonlit banana fields a hundred miles from the nearest city. "You can call Sweden from there," exclaims Matts.

The bus driver hammers the horn a few times to beckon passengers. Nobody appears. We rumble back to the junction, turn back onto the dirt road, and continue toward Yaviza.

After a few minutes we stop beside a concrete ranch house. Two children bounce off the bus into their parent's arms. We drive off. The Swedes and I are the only passengers left. Civilization is now far behind us. As we penetrate deeper into the Darien I feel like we're speeding toward the edge of the world.

*   *   *   *

Within a few hours the dirt track dwindles into a rocky path. Then I see lights ahead. We pull over in front of a blue concrete building that looks like a supply store.

"We don't go any farther," says the bus jockey.

"Is this Yaviza?" I ask.

"No. Yaviza is 25 kilometers more."

"Why don't we continue to Yaviza?" I demand. "This is the bus to Yaviza, isn't it?"

He offers the same reply. "The bus doesn't go any farther."

The jockey gestures toward a garage-like building beside the supply store. "There are rooms here where you can lodge tonight. It will cost only ten dollars for the three of you. In the morning you will find transport to Yaviza."

"How much will it cost to get to Yaviza from here," I ask.

"Five dollars each."

Matts starts cursing about the jockey in English. We slash five dollars each from the fare we were to pay him to Yaviza, giving him nine dollars each instead of fourteen.

After retrieving our bags from the roof, we get the key to our room, then trudge to our quarters and dump our bags on the floor. I walk back outside to the supply store and buy a machete for three dollars. When I return to the room the Swedes are reorganizing their backpacks. Considering I've spent most of the past two days sitting on buses, I decide to take a walk.

Through the darkness I saunter down the rocky road, thinking about my expedition through the Gap. After a few minutes I return to the room. We shut off the lights. Even though the jungle around us is bursting with nighttime howls, we quickly fall asleep.

*   *   *   *

The buzz of a chainsaw wakes us at dawn. We gobble some cheese and bananas in our room. Then we don our backpacks and walk outside.

We soon arrange a ride to Yaviza in a government pickup truck with lettering on the side that states "Official Use Only."

"You can pay me whatever you want," says the gracious driver.

We toss our packs atop some gas cans and chunks of wood, then we jump into the back. He fires up the engine and pulls onto the dirt path. A few seconds later the wind is whistling past our ears and we're hanging on like bronco riders as the driver careens down the twisty path to Yaviza.

After an hour I see some wooden houses ahead. We slow down. A few hundred yards later the path ends and the pickup truck stops. We jump out and pay the driver a few dollars each.

We are standing in Yaviza, the last outpost on the Pan-American Highway — the beginning of the Darien Gap. In front of us, across a murky river, the mighty rainforest rises in the sky and stretches south almost a hundred torturous miles before reaching the first town in South America.

Civilization behind us, I behold the challenge. The primitive power of the panorama sparks a shiver up my neck.

Before crossing the river to enter the Darien, we visit the army post, which is a scruffy concrete shack in the center of the village. A balding officer with two gold pens sprouting from his chest pocket greets us in English. Along the wall a collection of rusty machetes stands ready to enforce the law.

A local man also enters the army shack, but not until he carefully lays his machete on the grass outside. I soon wish that I had also left my machete outside; as soon as the officer sees it, he starts haggling with me to swap my brand-new blade for one of his ancient models. After conceding that I want to keep my machete, he examines our passports. Then he tells us that three other gringos passed through here a few days ago. None left any message for us, but we reckon one was Paul.

Yaviza is filled with English-speaking blacks, descendants of Caribbeans who migrated to Panama at the beginning of the century to work on banana plantations and the canal. As we amble through the village back to the river, everyone asks us where we're going. When we tell them we're planning to walk to Colombia they shake their heads in disbelief and declare, "You guys are crazy. There are much easier ways to get to Colombia than walking through the jungle."

As we reach the riverbank a skinny boy runs up to us. For a dollar he offers to ferry the three of us to the other side in his dugout. The Swedes go first. Then he poles back across the river for me. Very cautiously I step into the dugout. I'm now sitting in nothing more than a hollowed log. The opposite bank is about 40 feet away. I hope that we don't flip and send my backpack rushing downstream to be swallowed by the river.

With a shove from his pole, the boy sends us wobbling into the current. Straining all his little muscles, he maneuvers the dugout to the opposite shore. We bump into the boggy bank. I give him his dollar then climb out. Kneeling in the mud I hoist my pack. Then I slip and scramble up the first riverbank of the expedition.

Above the bank a path penetrates the rainforest. We take a last look at the village, the yellow pickup truck that carried us here, and the dirt track that marks the end of the Pan-American Highway. Then we turn around and walk into the jungle.

*   *   *   *

Our first destination marked on my sketchy map is a native village identified as Unión de Choco, about five hours of hiking from here. But after only a few minutes of walking along the trail I stop and call out to the Swedes. "Hey guys, wait a second. This makes no sense at all — we're supposed to be heading south into Colombia but my compass says we're heading north."

Getting lost after just a few minutes is a poor way to start an expedition. We stand baking in the heat, wondering what to do.

"Okay, guys," I finally say, "wait here with my pack. I'll run back to Yaviza and ask someone if this is the right trail. It's better to find out now instead of after hours of walking."

I ease my pack to the ground then start jogging back up the trail, carrying only my machete. Across the river from Yaviza I find a hut with some people lounging inside. They confirm that we're following the right trail and that it will veer south after a few more minutes. I turn around and pound back down the trail toward the Swedes. I'm pleased that we're heading in the right direction and that our adventure is beginning successfully. By the time I reach the Swedes I'm panting. "Yes. This is the proper trail."

"Good," says Matts, "let's continue walking."

Lined by bushes, the wide trail skirts the murky river. After a few minutes of trudging, I hear an ominous drone behind me that quickly rises to a deafening roar. We halt. Through the trees we see a bush plane skimming the river. Though she's flying at about 50 feet, the Darien's mighty trees tower like walls along each bank, rising another hundred feet above her. The plane evidently just took off from the airstrip in Yaviza. She whizzes past, finally surfaces above the trees, then soars north toward civilization.

Yaviza is still only a few minutes behind us. After walking a few hundred more feet, I look ahead on the trail and see two haggard white men stumbling toward us. "Hey mates!" they holler. "How ya doin'?" The men turn out to be two Australian adventurers who have spent the past two weeks exploring the rainforest. They tell us they haven't seen another white person since they began their excursion. Although they've spent half a month in the bush, they say they were merely roaming and hadn't intended to cross the Gap into Colombia. Now they're returning to Yaviza to look for transport back to Panama City.

While the Aussies and Swedes compare maps I decide to rest. I remove my pack (which feels like a load of lead bricks). Then I move to the side of the trail to crouch under some ferns and shun the blazing sun. I end up falling backward and sinking my butt into a patch of mud. Oh well, I'm already filthy. Besides, the mud is cool.

The Aussies continue up the trail to Yaviza. "Good luck on your expedition," they bellow. "And hey — watch you don't get caught in the rains."

We continue down the trail. In my right hand I'm clutching my machete. The new blade is shimmering in the morning light. Splashes of sweat drip from my face and splatter the dust. Within minutes my muddy rear dries. The path narrows. Yaviza is far behind us now. The trail becomes a dark, winding tunnel pierced by bird shrieks and fluttering with mystical purple butterflies.

FIRST RIVER VILLAGE

The muggy jungle tunnel rises and dips and winds around mammoth tree trunks. The path no longer follows the river, but every few minutes we meet a ravine. Because we're hiking through the dry season, the ravines are just mud-beds. We slide down each bank, trudge through muck for about ten feet, then grasp protruding roots to crawl up the opposite side.

While trying to climb from one ravine, my legs sink deeply into the mud. I strain to pull myself up, but the mud sucks me down. It takes about 20 seconds to pull free and haul myself and my heavy pack up the slippery bank. The mud reminds me of an admonition from my friends back in Toronto. When they discovered I was planning to hike through the jungle, they warned me to beware of quicksand. Hollywood quicksand, of course, swiftly devours you: the more you struggle, the quicker you sink; your sole hope is to snatch some trailing vine and pull yourself out. But Hollywood quicksand is a movie myth. Real quicksand is rare, and real quicksand is actually more buoyant than water, so it's difficult to sink into.

We pause to rest. I throw off my pack and lie on the ground. So far in my Latin American travels I've experienced heatstroke and dehydration. Even though I've been in Latin America three months now, I'm not acclimatized to today's grueling hike. The jungle has quickly drained my fluids. Untreated, a dehydrated jungle trekker soon experiences lethargy, followed in severe cases by coma, then death. Dehydration comes so quickly in the jungle heat that trekkers have died with water in their backpacks. I reach for my canteen and gulp most of my water.

After a few minutes we continue down the shaded trail. The hiking becomes a monotonous march — one foot in front of the other — step, step, step.... I try not to think about how many weeks I'll be spending here. Instead I think of every struggling footstep as one step closer to the next rest break, one step closer to our first camp, one step closer to luxurious South America with its roads and buses and restaurants and beds....

About an hour and a half after leaving Yaviza I hear water gurgling. Then I hear voices. The trail veers sharply right then falters, obstructed by bushes. We wrestle through the bushes and emerge in brilliant sunlight. We're standing on the banks of the Tuira River. The opposite shore is dotted with huts. We've reached the Afro-Panamanian village of Pinogana.

Across the river some little black boys see us and start yelling excitedly to the rest of the village. One boy jumps into a dugout and poles over to us. The Swedes give him a few coins and he ferries them across one at a time. When he returns for me I slide down the bank and try to slide right into the dugout without plopping my feet into the water. I slide into the boat successfully but its bottom is filled with swampy water so my feet become soaked anyway. When we reach the opposite shore I try clambering up the bank by grabbing tufts of grass and weeds, but they quickly break loose and send me sliding back into the river. By the time I ascend the slope, my hands, backpack and knees are covered in mud. Moreover I've left my machete amid the grasses on the opposite shore. Thankfully the dugout boy poles back across and retrieves it for me.

Matts and Urban are standing beside a big hut in the center of the village. We haven't yet penetrated the depths of Darien; the Pacific Coast is only about 50 miles downstream from this pioneer settlement. Pinogana has an electrical generator and several wires strung between some of the huts. Occasionally, one of the bigger dugouts motors upstream from the coastal towns with a few barrels of fuel. The people in the hut have even hauled a deep freezer upstream. They've wired the freezer to the generator to sell chilled soda to the villagers. The Swedes buy a few bottles of Coca-Cola to guzzle. I walk over to them and recline against the hut in the shade. Dozens of little boys crowd around to gawk at us. Some of them coax their sisters to come to see us, then they jokingly offer us the girls as wives.

I ask the woman in the hut whether many gringos pass through here. She says about three a week, but she describes them as Colombians, not pale white like us.

We don our packs once more and ask where the trail to Unión de Choco is. They point a few hundred feet upstream to a field beside the village. We march toward the field and find the trail. Once again we enter the dim and twisting tunnel.

THE CHOCO NATIVES

The trail veers away from the river and snakes upward. Pinogana is far behind us, and Yaviza is just a memory. It is now mid-morning. According to our sketchy directions, we should reach Unión de Choco by mid-afternoon.

My pants are trapping heat against my legs. I remove them and trek onward in my underwear. The bewildered Swedes stare at me. "You'll scratch the hell out of your legs," advises Urban.

"It's better than collapsing from heat exhaustion," I snap.

The path meanders wildly while steadily ascending rugged hills that provide an arduous climb with a heavy backpack. Toward noon the trail finally descends and once again skirts the Tuira River.

The path is well-trod here. Within a few minutes we discover a hut beside the river. Perched on stilts, the hut has a thick thatched roof and a sturdy floor, but no walls — like a raised gazebo made of logs and grass. Beside the hut stands a young Choco woman, tanned bronze and wrapped in a colorful hand-woven skirt and blouse. At first she seems shocked to see us. But when we say hello she smiles and greets us likewise.

We decide that this is a good place to break for lunch, so we sit alongside the trail beside the hut and get some food from our backpacks. The woman climbs a ladder into her hut and observes us.

After eating I ask the woman some questions. She speaks fluent Spanish. She says she is 18 years old and that she has visited Unión de Choco many times

45

because she used to go to a small school there that the Panamanian government built for the native children in this part of the jungle. I ask her how long it takes to walk from here to Unión de Choco. She contemplates the question for a few seconds, then tells me she doesn't know. I ask her whether it's about an hour, half an hour, a few minutes.... She contemplates again but offers the same answer. "I don't know." It's then that I realize that this woman doesn't comprehend time as we do. In fact she might never have seen a clock. I begin to understand that, in this timeless tropical wonderland, hours and minutes have little application. The jungle's inhabitants measure time with terms like dawn, midday, evening and night. No wonder she doesn't know how long it takes to reach Unión de Choco.

I'm thirsty but my canteen is now empty. I walk over to the riverside. "Can I drink the water from the river?" I ask the woman. She looks at me puzzled, trying to figure out my question.

"Where else would you get water to drink?" she replies. I quickly realize how odd my question must have sounded. Though I'm now in the jungle, my way of thinking is still in the city. I have to adapt my thinking to this environment ruled by nature. In the city our clock is a machine, our water comes from a faucet, and our food comes from a store shelf. In the jungle our clock is the sun, our water flows freely down the rivers and our food sprouts from the ground and the branches. I begin to realize that I'm now deep inside a different world.

We say goodbye to the woman and set off down the trail alongside the Tuira. The path becomes wide and flat and open to the sky. The Chocos have cleared parts of the rainforest to farm. We pass more huts, some of them surrounded by banana fields. Then the fields suddenly disappear and we penetrate a dark and skinny rainforest tunnel once more. But after about an hour the dense foliage diminishes and we emerge again among clusters of huts surrounded by banana fields. We pass several Choco men on the trail. They smile shyly. Most have heard about the gringos that occasionally visit the Darien.

The leafy banana trees cover both shorelines now. The river winds lazily through the fields. Suddenly, beside a cluster of huts, the path swerves to the left and descends straight into the river. We pause. "Where do we go now?" whines Matts.

As we sit down and consult my map, a boy beside one of the huts asks us where we want to go. "We are going to Unión de Choco," I tell him.

"Okay, wait a moment," he says. Then he runs down to the shore, heaves a dugout into the river and poles a few feet upstream to where we're sitting. "You have to cross the river to the path over there," he says. "I will bring you across in the dugout."

One by one he carries us across the water to the path. "Just follow this trail and it will take you to Unión." We thank him and continue hiking through the banana trees.

We've crossed the Tuira twice now, and both times I've stood in the water beside the boat and soaked my shoes. As I trek over the rugged ground with my 50-

47

pound pack, my wet feet shift around in my shoes. Soon my feet feel blistered and my footsteps begin to hurt.

After a few minutes we reach a junction in the path. After consulting our map we decide that the path to the left leads to Unión de Choco. We follow it. Soon the trail begins skirting the Tuira again, but now we're following the river downstream. This contradicts our hiking directions and, as the trail veers, it begins to contradict the proper compass bearing. But the path is getting wider. So we continue.

I keep looking up the path as we walk, but I see nothing but banana trees, banana trees and more banana trees. Then, as we round a curve in the path, I see a Choco hut, then another, then another. Soon we're standing in the middle of a primitive village.

The shocked natives gaze at us. Dozens of them quickly surround us. The women are covered around the waist with colorful cloths. A village elder approaches us cautiously. Blue dye decorates his face. Aside from a loincloth, he too is naked.

Not knowing what to do, I extend my hand to the elder in greeting. He shakes it. Then he shakes hands with the Swedes. Then everyone falls silent. The Chocos stare at us and we stare at them. I glance at the river and at the primitive habitations, then I hastily check my compass and the hiking directions. "Guys," I whisper to the Swedes, "I checked the hiking directions and, as far as I can tell, we've wandered off course — this is not Unión de Choco."

A SECOND EXPEDITION TEAM, AND PAUL

The Swedes agree that this doesn't seem to be Unión. We ask the elder what this village is called. He utters a baffling muddle of vowels. We mention the name Unión de Choco and he nods his head and gestures behind one of the huts to a narrow path into a banana field. We thank him and walk toward the path. I feel like snapping a few photos but I know the camera would be obtrusive. Some Latin American natives shun photographs because they believe that the camera steals your soul to make the picture.

Soon banana trees surround us again and the village is behind us. Late afternoon is approaching. We reckon Unión lies about an hour in front of us.

The path meanders through the banana groves, then straightens and widens. The Swedes start walking faster. I stop. "You guys go ahead. I'm gonna stop for a couple of minutes. My feet are killing me."

The Swedes stare at me for a few seconds with a trace of impertinence. "Okay, we'll keep going if you want. We'll see you in a few minutes in Unión."

With aching arms I remove my loaded pack from my sore back. Then I lie on the trail and remove my damp shoes. Blisters cover my toes and soles. I let the breeze dry my feet, then I replace my shoes and get up. Walking has become very painful. But I push forward. I keep repeating to myself that Unión is probably just a few hundred feet ahead of me. At the same time I'm angry at these blisters that are already hindering my expedition.

After about half a mile I hear children's voices, then I see an open field. Beyond the field, beside the Tuira, several dozen huts perch above the banana trees. I've made it to Unión de Choco, my first camp on my Darien expedition.

The Swedes walk out from the cluster of huts. "Come on over this way. We've already found a place to stay. And guess what — Paul and a couple of other gringos are here."

I follow the Swedes past the huts to a battered wooden shack. I learn later that the shack was built a few years ago by the Panamanian government as a goodwill gesture to the local natives. Painted on the wall of the shack is the slogan:

1986
YEAR OF PEACE
SECURITY WITHOUT WAR
GENERAL NORIEGA

Sitting on the porch is Paul. Standing beside him is a tall Danish traveler I roomed with in the hostel in San José. (So few gringos travel through Central America that one isn't surprised to meet the same traveler several times in several different countries. To meet someone here in the jungle, of course, is a bit less common.)

"So you got my messages," says Paul, smiling.

"We sure did," I respond, "but we didn't think we'd catch up to you."

I ease my pack to the ground. Then I wander over to the riverbank where I meet the third member of

Paul's expedition team — a ragged, long-haired American called Walter. With the two expedition teams combined, we have six gringos in the village: two lanky Swedes in their early 20s; the balding British professor Paul in his early 40s; the tall Dane in his early 30s; ragged Walter the American in his mid-20s; and me, Andrew the Canadian, the youngest of the six expeditioners at age 18.

The American and Dane met Paul shortly before starting their Darien exploit, and the three of them decided to challenge the Gap together. Unlike the Swedes and me who hiked here, the three journeyed to Unión by motor-dugout.

When I was back in Canada planning my Latin America journey, I envisioned crossing the Darien solo. In fact, aside from the two Swedes, all of us are solo travelers. But we each hold the same goal — to bridge the Gap. And it looks like our common goal has joined us together into one loosely-bound expedition team.

*   *   *   *

I shuffle around the village. From within their huts the shy Chocos peer at me. I buy a watermelon from one family. A platoon of children trails a few feet behind me. Like the adults, they're clad only in shorts.

Myriad necklaces of beads and animal fangs adorn almost every neck in the village. Blue dye covers their bodies. Derived from a plant called Jagua, the dye used for the body art, according to some beliefs, also discourages sunburn and mosquito bites.

51

By the riverbank stands a wooden shack that sells cans of food that have been ferried upstream on the Tuira. A few concrete sidewalk blocks line the edge of the river, probably laid down to make walking less muddy during the rainy season. Beside the field is a small concrete building, evidently the school built by the Panamanian government.

When I return to the hut, Paul is standing beside a chubby Choco man with a bowl haircut. "This is the chief, Andrew. You should ask him if it's alright for you to stay in his village for a few days."

The chief speaks fluent Spanish. He says I'm welcome to stay. Paul advises me to give him a dollar later, as the other expeditioners already have, for graciously accommodating us. After a few minutes of standing with us, occasionally muttering a few words, the chubby chief politely excuses himself and joins the children who are gawking at Paul's pup tent. He seems more comfortable observing us than conversing with us.

I walk over to the Dane, who is chatting with a man in a loincloth hewing a log into a dugout. The muscular little Choco asks whether we have children. The Dane says no. Then he asks whether we at least have women. Once again the Dane replies no. "You don't even have women with you? You poor men," he sighs.

Evening is approaching. I return to the hut. Encircled by an audience of curious children, Walter is preparing his supper on the porch. I ask him of his travels. He tells me he's been trekking through Central America for two years now, much of that time living with natives. Then he turns to me and proclaims,

"There's too many of us gringos here. These Chocos have been friendly so far, but they're starting to feel threatened, man, like we're taking over their village. It's a good thing we're leaving here tomorrow. Otherwise they might start to worry."

I climb onto the porch (the steps are broken) then recline against the wall and start eating the watermelon that I just bought. My blisters still hurt and I don't want to move my weary body. In fact I'm so tired that I feel like staying here until the rainy season starts at the end of the month.

I ask the curious children what they think of Noriega. "Noriega is Noriega and he is bad," they reply.

"Why is he bad?" I ask.

"He is bad because he is bad," they reason. Then one of the children points at Matts and adds, "and he looks like Noriega's son."

I withdraw some beans from my pack and eat my evening meal. Night gradually encroaches. The aroma of cooking fires and boiling rice fills my lungs. On the other bank of the Tuira, the banana trees wallow in the lazy breeze. Beyond the banana fields the western highlands rise, uninhabited by humans, the realm of savage beasts.

*   *   *   *

Darkness finally descends over the Darien Rainforest. An oil lamp illuminates the interior of the large communal meeting hut in the center of the village, where several of the elders are playing a table game and drinking the corn beer that the villagers make.

I enter our shack, stumble around the holes in the floor, then erect my hammock beside Matts'. Although I bought the hammock before I traveled to Latin America, tonight is my first time using it. My first attempt to lie in it tosses me to the floor. But my second try proves successful. The others string their hammocks over the porch. Paul retires to his pup tent.

Outside the shack, the jungle creatures begin their nocturnal shrieking and howling. The hammock sways through the muggy air and I drift asleep.

THE EXPEDITION DEPARTS WITHOUT ME

Morning sun pierces the cracked walls of the shack and slices the dusty air. The shrieks and howls of the rainforest faded with the arrival of dawn. Now the buzz of Chocos making breakfast saturates the air.

Outside the shack, Paul is dismantling his tent. He removes the poles one by one and arranges them in a bundle. (The chief didn't ask Paul to pay a dollar for lodging in his village because he brought his own little house.) One of the young onlookers from last night returns to watch the gringos. He scrutinizes Paul's tent poles and remarks that we have a fine set of fish spears.

The chief soon arrives and greets us warmly with an incomprehensible expression. Walter smiles at me. "He's speaking Old Spanish. He asked 'How did you dawn?'."

To assure the chief that I slept well during my first night in his village I reply that I dawned fine (though my first experience snoozing eight hours in my ten-dollar hammock unpleasantly contorted my body by morning).

Walter is now stooped over and scouring the ground beside the shack, pausing every few seconds to pluck a weed. I watch curiously. When he has a handful of the leaves he returns to the porch. "These are great weeds," he discloses. "Whenever I find them I collect them to shred into my cereal."

The other expeditioners are cooking oatmeal on their portable stoves. To save weight and money I'm trekking Darien with no stove, no pots, not even a fork or spoon. I simply use my hands or slurp.

After eating I hobble down to the river like an old man. The blisters on my feet feel worse today. I survey the morning bustle and then return to the shack. The others are packing their knapsacks and preparing to leave. Unlike me, these five want to rush across the Gap. I want to wander through the Darien more slowly to deeply experience life in the rainforest. I decide to stay here in Unión de Choco for a few days to mend my feet and to learn from the natives. Besides, it's not as though the five will be first to cross the Gap; every year several adventurers hike from Panama to Colombia through Darien.

Soon the five assemble in front of the shack. They tie their boots and adjust their backpack straps and stroke the sharpening stone along their machetes a few last times. Then they wave goodbye and march through the village toward the riverside trail and soon disappear beyond a patch of coconut trees.

I stand barefoot on the porch while surveying my surroundings — the perched huts with drooping roofs, the tall corn stalks rustling in the breeze and the glistening river rushing through the jungle toward the Pacific. Although the village brims with friendly natives, and although I've spent the past three months traveling solo through war zones and urban slums, I now feel very alone, like my first day of kindergarten when my dad brought me up the road to the elementary school and deposited me in a classroom of strangers.

*   *   *   *

Reclining on the porch, I scrutinize the village, this tiny settlement in the vast rainforest, a speck of lint on a lavish green sweater. Aside from the chief, the adults in the village observe me from a distance. The little girls are also too shy to visit the gringo. But the little boys perpetually surround me — thirteen now cover the porch, some spilling over its edges, others sprawled across my lap and looking up into my face. Any movement and any word fascinates them. I ask them questions — what do you think of the jungle, what do you think of Panama, what do you know about other countries in the world? I learn that only one of the 13 boys has journeyed beyond the rainforest; he once went to Panama City to visit his brother.

I walk over to examine the small concrete school. The school is the only building in the village with a lock on the door (it's closed for vacations). The building is divided into five small rooms. Inside each section is a simple teacher's desk that faces a few dozen smaller desks. Each section also has a mural. One mural depicts a map of Panama with some children standing by a riverbank. Another mural pictures a man carrying bananas through the jungle. When I ask the boys what they learn here, they say, "a lot of health, plus some reading and writing."

About noon the boys decide to go elsewhere. Several of them start wrestling. Others retrieve their slingshots to hurl mangoes, practicing the hunting skills they'll need when they're older.

I move my hammock to the more secluded back porch and sway from side to side while watching the sugarcane fields shifting in the sultry breeze. The suffocating midday heat has silenced the village into its daily siesta. One boy returns from the river. With four jugs draped around his neck he deftly climbs the ladder into his hut, then empties the jugs into a barrel. The sun is so scorching that the air above the barrel becomes misty as the water evaporates.

Suddenly the knot in my hammock rope slips and I drop to the floor. The fall jars me from my relaxation. I stand up and decide to roam through the village and down to the river.

Most villagers are dozing on the floors of their huts. One young mother lays her baby in a hammock and gives it an enduring swing, so forcefully in fact that she nearly launches the baby into the roof. But such a lasting swing calms the baby into a sleep and allows the mother to lie down and take a nap herself as the child continues to rock from side to side.

I descend a set of rickety steps to the river's edge. Several large dugouts are tied to the bank, lying low in the water under bulging sacks of green bananas. Beside the steps stand more jugs with their water evaporating before my eyes.

After washing my hands and face I return to the hut to inspect my feet. I remove my ragged socks. The soles of my feet are peeling. Two blisters are bulging on my left foot. Two more blisters are bulging in the same spot on my right foot. I decide that I'll have to pop them if I want to resume my expedition.

Some of the boys reappear and ask what I'm doing. I tell them I have a problem with my feet that I have to repair. I retrieve a safety pin from my pack and dip it into the bleach I use for sterilizing my drinking water.

Like a wounded soldier performing makeshift surgery, I lance the first blister. After stabbing deep holes in each bubble, I squeeze. White puss oozes out. The puss trickles down my foot, mixes with dirt and turns to mud. After cleaning and bandaging, I try hobbling around the village once more. The operation has slightly curtailed the pain.

The Chocos wake from their siesta. A woman beside the shack starts slicing the grass around her hut with a machete to ensure a neat lawn. Some of the natives look at me with surprise; they didn't realize that one of yesterday's gringos is still in their village.

I visit the riverside shack that sells supplies. Coconut trees and wild rose bushes surround the skimpy wood-board walls, along with several young men with early-Beatles haircuts like the chief. The shelves inside boast notebooks, canned sardines and Vicks VapoRub, all goaded upriver on the dugouts. I buy a can of beans. As in the rest of Panama, the currency here is the United States dollar. My change is an American quarter that reads "26 July 1969 In Remembrance of Successful Moon Landing."

I buy a watermelon and return to my back porch. As I eat the melon, its juice dribbles down my arms and soaks my pants. And I have to keep shuffling to different parts of the porch to flee the ravenous ants that assail me to share my snack.

Some of the boys return to observe me. Necklaces of jaguar fangs dangle across their bony, bronze chests. When I ask them where they got the teeth they narrate sensational stories about their fathers' hunting kills. I decide to spend as much time as possible during the

next few days interacting with these captivating
natives.

THE FASCINATING VILLAGERS

As dinnertime approaches, the afternoon heat fades into a pleasant breeze. Barefoot and bare-chested, I'm beginning to look like the Chocos here, except I haven't brushed my teeth or washed for a few days so I'm much grubbier than they are. I banish my laziness and, soap in hand, meander to the river to bathe.

The fading sun casts a warm glow on the tall earthy banks. I strip to my underwear and step into the gooey river bottom. I keep the soap in my hand — I don't want to place it atop one of the many rocks in case the rock has legs and decides to walk away. It feels odd to get my feet so muddy considering I'm entering the river to become clean. But I dunk myself in the rushing water and scrub away yesterday's grueling hike.

I try to paddle a few feet upstream. As I swim with all my might against the Tuira's current, I remain stationary. After washing my hair, I recline in the frothy rapids under a swaying palm tree. Along the shore, the banana-laden dugouts bob in the current. Every few minutes a floating mango dashes past me downstream. And every few seconds I feel a fish nip my toes. Surging through the delicate ecosystem, these immense volumes of water are the lifeblood of Darien.

Two boys shove a small dugout into the water to take it for a spin, as in my country teenagers borrow the family car. Then I hear a rustling sound beside me in the foliage. Stalking behind some reeds, two giggling children are spitting berries at me with a blowgun. Their amusement quickly expires when a woman appears on top of the bank and hollers, "Come up here for dinner right now."

I emerge from the river and check my face in a pocket mirror I haven't used since I began my Darien crossing. A shocking wild man stares back at me. I shave. Then, feeling fresher, I stroll back to the shack.

* * * *

I have inhabited the rainforest for only two days, but my way of thinking is already conforming to my new environment. Like the Choco woman I met along the trail yesterday, my mind is losing its tendency to function in hours and minutes. As far as I'm concerned, it's just a warm, peaceful evening in the dry season.

In the west the sun is hovering above the distant chain of mountains. A throbbing orb, she rolls a glowing orange carpet over the endless broccoli-like canopy. Then she descends behind the highlands, leaving a flaming red horizon cut jagged by the bulging mountains.

Thin columns of smoke rise throughout the village as the women kindle the dinner fires. Soon the malarial mosquitoes start buzzing through the village. These mosquitoes appear mainly at dawn and dusk. My white shirt protects me somewhat because the mosquitoes generally won't land on light-colored clothing. Unlike most jungle trekkers, I'm not taking anti-malarial medication. I've heard worse reports about the side-effects than about the disease.

I check my watermelon for ants. Finding none, I decide to smush it into watermelon juice. Some boys that are watching me grab the discarded shell to gnaw. As I sit on the porch drinking my watermelon nectar, three women approach me and shake my hand. "Can you please tell us," asks one, "why you would want to go to Colombia?"

As I detail my expedition aspirations to the women, the chief emerges and shakes hands with me. Because I'm now shaven and clean and covered in different clothes, he thinks I'm a new gringo in his village. (These natives probably think all of us whites look the same.) Only after I explain that I've been here since yesterday does he recognize me. "But what happened?" he asks. "Why didn't you travel with your companions this morning?"

I explain that I would like to remain here a few more days to study his village. He assures me that he will be pleased to have me, although he shyly adds that he'd appreciate a dollar bill for each night I stay. He then tells me that another gringo once stayed with his people. He describes him as an American soldier from Monterey, California who lived with the Choco and even learned their language. When the chief finishes his story, he excuses himself to go to his hut for the evening meal.

After the chief walks away, the three women resume chatting with me. With them is a little girl wearing a beaded necklace with a coin for a pendant. The coin has worn smooth over the years, but when I lean down to her to examine it more closely, I notice the imprints "Republica de Colombia" and "1872." Back when the coin was minted, this village lay inside the Panama that was then just a remote Colombian province. I fetch a colorful cigarette lighter from my pack and offer to exchange it for the necklace. The girl accepts. The necklace isn't actually worth much more than the lighter, but it's an attractive memento for me of the jungle village.

My bartering amuses the three women. They tell me to try on my new necklace. I try, but it doesn't fit around my head and I drop it. As I bend down to pick it up, the three women reach out and stroke my hair to see what it feels like. "Hey, stop," I stammer, "what are you doing."

The women laugh, then they resume inspecting me. "Look at his eyes," exclaims one. "They're green." The three of them shove their faces into me to analyze my eyeballs. "Green eyes see better in the jungle and farther," they conclude.

I ask the women about their religious beliefs. "Most in the village are Christians," they explain, "but we still use our witch doctor." The women also tell me that many of the men take multiple wives, sometimes as many as five, often as young as 12 years old.

I ask the women whether someone could cook my food for me tonight. They say of course and they tell me to bring my food and follow them. I retrieve my bag of oatmeal from my knapsack and follow the women to a large hut in the middle of the village.

Climbing the five-foot high log ladder takes acrobatic dexterity, but I ascend it without flipping. The women seat me in the center of the hut in front of a table. On top of the table an oil lamp burns steadily, illuminating the faces of several men sitting across from me. The men welcome me to their home. In the darkness, around the edge of the hut, several others are lounging in hammocks. Occasional flickers from the lamp reveal their watchful gaze.

The women prepare enough oatmeal to provide a portion for everyone here. As we eat, the men ask me about my homeland. After listening to me, they tell me that even though I'm a world traveler I should return to their village one day and they'll give me a woman.

I ask the men whether piranhas swim in these rivers. "Of course," they say. One of the men says piranhas have attacked him several times. He turns around and exposes deep scars covering his back. We continue discussing the piranhas, although every few minutes the conversation is interrupted when one of the natives passes gas, which propels the others into convulsions of laughter.

I ask the natives about their language. They try to teach me a word, but I just can't make my mouth say it and they launch into more convulsions of laughter.

The people of this hut display more prosperity than the other villagers, owning such gadgets as a portable radio. Several foreign missionaries broadcast programs to this part of Panama to try to convert the natives on Darien's populated Caribbean coast. Even these Choco living deep in the rainforest can hear some of the broadcasts. The program they're receiving features a woman reciting Catholic prayers with little children repeating her words. The natives say they'll try to find a broadcast in English for me. After fiddling with the tuning knob they find a program with English lessons. A monotone voice repeats "You are a good student" followed by "You didn't call me yesterday" then "Oil is used for frying" and finally "Happiness is wonderful."

The natives shift the conversation to the dangers of traveling to Colombia. They tell me that bandits and the Colombian rebels hide along the jungle trails. "They will kill you for your money in that country," warns one. "Once you pass into Colombian territory you face great danger. Just last year two trekkers like you were killed by the guerillas." The men go on to tell stories of the guerillas' murdered victims floating down the rivers of the jungle.

Our conversation has drifted several hours into the night, and most of the villagers are now settling down to sleep. I thank my hosts for the dinner and excuse myself to return to my shack.

*   *   *   *

I recline in my hammock and sway in the darkness. My flashlight and switchblade lie close beside me, a habit I established to protect myself in all the sleazy four-dollar-a-night hostels I've lodged in for the past three months.

As I'm drifting asleep I hear the village's pack of dogs growling outside the shack. Then they erupt with savage infighting. For a few seconds the night echoes with vicious snarling and yelping, then the dogs scatter, leaving only the chattering and squawking of the jungle. Throughout Latin America I've frequently observed clusters of strays rummaging through garbage together, then suddenly exploding in vicious fighting (to the delight of bystanders who applaud the fracas.)

As I swing gently, I decide that the beams that my hammock is tied to are so close together that the hammock hangs too curved for comfort, so I carry it outside and string it between the porch railings.

Like a steamy sauna with the lights off, the night air exudes fragrant humidity. I strip to my underwear and stretch out on the nylon webbing. Sweat dribbles off my skin, but I fall into a deep slumber.

Throughout the night the suffocating heat slowly rises from the jungle and dissipates into the star-speckled sky. At about midnight I wake feeling cool. I put on my trousers and shirt. A few hours later I wake once more, this time even cooler. I don my sweatshirt and windbreaker; but not until I cover my face with my towel do I resume my sleep in warmth.

THUNDER OVER THE BANANA FIELDS

The jungle is silent when my eyes open. A dreamy mist shrouds the banana trees in the half-light of dawn. The only sound in the village is the melody of a mother singing to her baby.

The long shadows gradually shorten and soon the flaming sun emerges above the treetops and begins to bake the jungle. Two discoveries prompt me to get out of bed: first, I've twisted myself into such a peculiar posture during the night that I'm on the verge of flipping out of my hammock and onto the floor; second, I notice a beehive buzzing in the mango tree beside my head.

As I disentangle myself from the hammock, the chief emerges and greets me. Shortly afterward, one of the men I shared dinner with last night arrives and asks, "Are you not coming to eat breakfast?"

I bring my bag of oatmeal to the hut once more and together we make breakfast. Although we make a mess, the oatmeal tastes splendid once we pick out the bugs.

The conversation during this meal focuses on the walking time to various settlements. The men tell me how many hours I must trek to reach the other villages on my expedition route. They know that a half-day of hiking up the Tuira will bring me to my next destination, the Afro-Panamanian village named Boca de Cupe. But a few miles past Boca de Cupe the Choco domain ends. Of the land beyond they know only that it is ruled by the Kuna tribe, their traditional enemy.

The men then ask me about walking distances to places I'm familiar with. "How many hours walk is it from here to America?" asks one. He seems shocked when I tell him how distant America is, so he tries another question. "Well, then, how many hours is it from here to Germany?" He seems even more shocked when I tell him that Germany is across the ocean. Another man asks about Panama's neighboring countries. "Do they speak Spanish in Honduras and Costa Rica?"

Toward the end of breakfast the natives become intrigued when they discover I have underarm hair, and they ask me to raise my arms so they can inspect me.

The man who invited me to breakfast finishes his oatmeal, then pushes his bowl aside and reclines to let his food settle. With gratitude he looks at me and says, "For sharing that oatmeal with us you deserve four women."

I finish my breakfast and return to my home on the back porch of the shack, wondering why I see so few villagers this morning. The boys are taking turns swinging in my hammock. When I ask them where all their parents have gone they tell me that their parents have hiked to another village today to trade.

*   *   *   *

Swinging in my hammock, I notice that the sky has grown overcast. The clouds rumble and a warm drizzle begins to fall. The rain cleanses the dusty jungle and fills my nostrils with a fruity fragrance that reminds me of childhood days picking raspberries. But within half an hour the drizzle ends and the sun reappears and steams the damp soil.

The chief comes to visit me on the back porch to ask me for my impressions of his village. As we chat, a mechanical flutter rumbles from the southern edge of the village. Quickly surging toward the shack, the rumble becomes a roar. Then suddenly, a few dozen feet above the porch, a green army helicopter rushes past us, banks over the banana trees, and descends on the field beside the school.

The chief leaps off the porch and dashes with the rest of the villagers to the field. I grab my camera and notebook and follow him. When I reach the field, the chopper blades are slowly slapping the air. I stand at a distance as two men and a woman climb out. The chief walks up to greet them. "We'd like to hold a short health meeting for the women," says the man.

The chief escorts the visitors to the meeting hut where the women assemble. The men return to their chores. They tell me that a helicopter with government people visits the village every few months to hold some kind of health meeting.

Meanwhile the boys crowd around the chopper. One of the men from the helicopter stands beside the pilot and scans the village. His head slowly swivels and his eyes warily absorb the primeval surroundings — his gaze falls on the skimpy huts, the rustling corn stalks, the playful dark-skinned little humans, then his gaze suddenly stops to behold a tall, paler human with ragged clothes and a beaded necklace, and his face wrinkles in confusion. "Hey!" he cries, pointing at me. "Come over here."

I walk over to the man. "What are you doing here?" he demands.

"Well, I'm traveling through the Darien to go to Colombia."

"I see," he replies with a look of fascination. Then he walks off.

One of the young Choco men starts chatting with me. "Our chief no longer has any authority because the other people have the flying machines." He also tells me that in Colombia "is nothing." An elderly woman with deflated breasts standing beside him disagrees. "No, Colombia is full of killers."

A few minutes later, the officials return from the health meeting and climb back through the chopper's side door. The pilot starts the turbine engines. The blades smack the air and blow the banana trees until they bend over and, like a bulging green insect, she slowly lifts above the field and thunders away over the treetops to her northern base.

* * * *

I return to the shack and take out some cans of food. As usual, several of the villagers come to watch me. They marvel that I have beans sealed inside a can (though I bought some in their village). When they see me pull out a foot-long spiced sausage they roar with laughter and tell the other villagers to come and look.

By now the villagers are accustomed to me. Several of the adults visit me to chat. Most want to learn about the outside world. I tell one man that in the outside world a man can get a medical operation to change him into a woman. The news bewilders him. Then I tell him that in the outside world some men have sex with other men and some women have sex with other women. He stares at me in shock. He tells me that he knows little about the ways of the outside world, but he says that some women of this village travel to a resort on the edge of the jungle where they earn 14 dollars if they dance with no shirts.

Compared to many in the developing world, the natives in this village beam with health. Their fields flourish with bananas, coconuts and corn. Abundant mangoes and other fruits dangle from the trees. The rivers teem with fish.

Unfortunately, if one of the natives does become ill, proper medical care is non-existent and death can follow quickly. One young girl standing beside the shack looks like a one-year-old but her mother tells me she is three. She suffers from a bloated belly and wiry arms that are not much thicker than my thumb. I look into her motionless black eyes. "She can walk a bit," her mother remarks, "but she has been sick since birth — in the past month she has gotten much worse." I lift the child and hold her close to me. She is a delicate feather. But they might have already prepared her grave.

*   *   *   *

The sunset once again paints the western sky orange. Then it dwindles into midnight blue. When the sun rises in the morning, I will leave Unión de Choco and resume my trek toward Colombia. As with all the other towns and villages I've explored for the last three months, I'll probably never return here.

My next destination is an Afro-Panamanian village named Boca de Cupe, a few hours hike upstream along the Tuira. I still don't know how long it will take me to bridge the Gap and reach South America.

With my bag of oatmeal I once again visit my dinner hut. The women seat me in my usual chair. I tell them that I will continue toward Colombia in the morning. "But we don't want you to leave," they urge. "You can stay with us in our village." I thank them but decline, explaining that I must leave for Colombia and soon return to my homeland.

During this evening's meal the natives interrogate me about the populations of various nations. They can't comprehend that Canada has 25 million people when Panama has only four million. They sit silent, momentarily stunned. I don't even consider mentioning China's 1000 million people — such a figure might overwhelm them.

Throughout our conversation a vampire bat is whizzing around us. "Don't worry, he won't kill us," says one man. "He's just here to suck our blood." Soon a second bat arrives and one of the boys runs after them to shoo them away.

The women place on the table several fish with crunchy skin and meat that tastes like chicken. "What kind of fish are these?" I ask.

"They are the ones that were biting you in the river," they answer.

After we finish eating, the women take the dishes away. The man across from me leans toward me with a solemn expression, his eyes flickering from the flame of the oil lamp. He strives to explain what I've got myself into. "Listen. Your journey to Colombia will be so difficult. Do you not realize that for the remainder of your route you will not encounter any train or bus whatsoever — you will have to walk and take riverboats the whole way."

I assure him that I already know this and that I'm prepared to continue my excursion. He wishes me well, satisfied that he has at least warned me about my perilous pursuit.

We chat for a few more hours, then I thank them for the meal and excuse myself. I stumble through the pitch-dark village searching for my home. When I think I'm close I flick on my flashlight and it illuminates my little white house.

After fixing my hammock on the back porch, I roam around outside the shack. Across the river a pack of monkeys howls in the treetops. I lie in the grass for a few minutes and gaze at the heavens, from horizon to horizon spilling over with countless shimmering galaxies. Then I return to my hammock and drift asleep.

Dawn rises, but I try to sleep for a few extra hours. Just like the other nights, the jungle heat steadily dissipated and I kept waking and donning more and more clothes, finally succumbing once again to covering my face with my towel to keep warm.

As I try to sleep, I hear footsteps walking through the shack and then walking out onto the porch and stopping beside me. I feel a gaze hovering above me. I inch back the towel and peek out with one eye. The chief is staring down at me. "Are you cold?" he asks.

"No. I'm not cold now."

"My, you have such a small hammock," he remarks. Then he tells me why he has come to visit. "I came to tell you that some of us are traveling upstream to Boca de Cupe this morning."

"When?"

"We are just about to leave. We will fetch you when we're ready to depart."

The chief walks off. I gather my belongings, don my walking shoes, and repack my knapsack. Then I wander around searching for the chief, but I can't find him. I visit the chief's house. They say he is not around and that they don't know of any boats heading upstream today. I march to the riverside. All the dugouts have disappeared.

An annoying tendency of these natives is their unreliability in some matters. They might have already embarked. They might have forgotten to tell me that they were leaving. They might have changed their minds and decided to go upstream later on, or tomorrow, or next week. I reckon that I could wait days to secure a boat ride to Boca de Cupe, so I decide to start trekking.

I hoist my backpack and clasp my machete. Then I slowly walk through the village, saying farewell to the people who have treated me so kindly.

The boys are dashing around playing games. One of the men I met the first day is walking toward a trail behind my shack to go hunting for panther and wild pig. His waist is girded with a loincloth that bounces on his buttocks with each stride.

When I reach the southern edge of Unión I take a last look at the drooping huts and the breakfast fires and the bare-breasted women dyed blue and adorned with beaded necklaces. Then I turn around and embark down the thin, bumpy trail.

To my right the Tuira is rushing over the rocks. The omnipresent banana trees surround me; their wide leaves swishing in the early morning breeze. I should reach Boca de Cupe by early afternoon.

DEEPER INTO DARIEN

The banana trees soon diminish, overwhelmed by rashes of overgrowth and towering trees. Within a few minutes the suffocating heat compels me to stop.

I sit on my pack. The first few minutes after you pause to rest are the hottest: your body still swelters, but the gentle breeze from walking vanishes, so the sweat flows.

I wade into the river to cool my feet. But the Tuira caresses my legs so refreshingly that I decide to jump in for a swim. After splashing around in the shallows I brush my teeth and shave, then I put on my clothes and sit on a boulder.

As I'm about to stand up to resume hiking I hear a buzzing downriver. The buzzing grows and two motorized dugouts zoom around the corner and point upstream toward me. I wave my hand — why walk to Boca when I can hitch a riverboat? The first dugout whizzes past. The second dugout slows and pulls over beside me. The two men sitting in the boat look at me, probably wondering why I'm here and what I want. Short and dark-skinned, they might be natives, though they don't look like the Choco I've just been living among. "I'll give you a dollar to carry me to Boca de Cupe," I offer.

One of the men nods his head and motions me to climb in. I grab my pack and lower it into the boat. Then I clamber in. The sternsman lowers the Johnson outboard into the water and guns it. We accelerate upstream.

The river widens and deepens. The sternsman revs the motor and we surge over the water, swerving around rocks and logs. Watching for obstructions, the bowman up front blares warnings. "Rock left!" "Log right!" "Sandbar ahead!" With dolphin-like agility we whip around the obstacles.

Over the shallows he lifts the outboard from the water, spraying silver sheets into the wind. Then through the deep water he lowers the prop again and nails it.

The speeding dugout splits the river into cascades of froth. Silver droplets fling into my lap. We fly upriver. All the while I'm grasping the gunwales and sitting backward because that's the way I stepped into the thing.

A banana grove appears beside us alongside a lengthy sandbar. Then several huts appear amidst the trees. A half-dozen young black boys run down from the huts and sprint along the sandbar trying to race us. When the sandbar descends into the river the boys skid to a halt.

We round a bend and I see several dugouts alongside the bank and a half-dozen men fishing. As we whiz past, one of the men sees me and waves. It's the chief! So they did travel upriver today.

We cruise for a while at a steady hum. Then the river narrows and we approach a rapids. He guns it, then lifts the engine. I hang on, waiting to hit the rapids. Pause, then SPLASH! We smack the whitecap and a second later blast out the other side. Once again he lowers the engine and revs it.

Because we're at the end of the dry season the Tuira is running shallow. We slow down again and he lifts the engine. The bowman poles us through, pushing against the rocky bottom, then lifting his great stick, which dribbles brown water off its tip into the boat. Foot by foot we push upstream until the water deepens again. Then we resume motoring, picking up speed till we're soaring once more. Suddenly the bowman yells, "To the right! To the right! Sandbar!"

Heading straight into the bar at high speed we swerve madly. CRASH! The keel smashes the sand. But our momentum carries us over the obstacle and we splash back into the current and continue upstream.

Soon we pass a mossy green island. A few hundred feet farther, in the middle of the river, stands a gargantuan dead tree tanned by a hundred summers, crowned by a great black jungle bird — a statue of tribute to the mighty Darien.

Against a backdrop of monster trees, the shores once again become speckled with banana trees and sugarcane. Thin trails lead up from the riverside to ragged huts atop the bank. Ahead on the river an old black man is poling upstream in a tiny dugout. He nods a greeting as we pass.

The river becomes shallow once more. Up ahead more whitewater bubbles. The sternsman accelerates, then lifts the prop. We ram the rapids. Blobs of green water plop into my lap. The bowman looks back — with an anxious expression he frantically barks directions. We pole through and, a few seconds later, drift out the other side.

The water deepens. The sternsman lowers the prop and we continue upriver. A few minutes later we round a bend and approach a group of riverboats tied up on the eastern bank. Atop the bank is a line of shacks. We run up on a sandbar beside the other dugouts. The sternsman turns to me. "We're at Boca de Cupe."

* * * *

We step onto the shore. I pull a dollar from my money belt and present it to the sternsman. He looks at it for a second, then looks back at me. "What's that?" he scowls.

"It's the dollar I said I'd pay you to carry me to Boca."

"What about gasoline?" he says.

"You never mentioned anything about gasoline."

"Of course you have to contribute toward gasoline as well," he persists.

I start to feel that this guy is trying to scam me. "Okay, how much is it with gasoline," I ask.

"Twelve dollars, no less," he demands.

"Twelve dollars! You agreed to one dollar to carry me to Boca de Cupe and now you're asking for 12? No. I won't pay you 12." I reach into my money belt. "Here. I'll give you four, no more."

The men realize that I know they're trying to scam me. Sensing that further bartering with me is pointless, they reluctantly accept the four dollars.

I climb the 20 feet of muddy shoreline and emerge on a concrete sidewalk. With the Pacific Ocean still only a few hours downstream, even this village shows signs of the modern world. A few dozen wooden shacks line the concrete path. Several of the shacks beam colorfully, some painted pink, others yellow, some sky blue. Another bigger shack in the center of the village serves as a supply store. Just as in Pinogana, Boca de Cupe has a mini generator that the villagers run for a few hours each day to produce electricity.

I walk over to the store. My guidebook says that I have to show my passport there to the proprietor, who notes my name in an immigration register for the government. When I walk into the shop the man behind the counter looks at me with an expression that says, "Aha, another crazy Darien adventurer." He asks for my passport and gives me a form to fill out. Ferried upstream occasionally from Panama City, such forms are long and complex and out of character with the casual jungle village. After I complete the form he hands me the register. I see Matts's name from two days ago. I sign the register and he returns my passport, complete with an exit stamp. The exit stamp reinforces to me that Boca de Cupe is like a last tiny bastion of civilization before the deep, expansive wilderness.

I wander back outside. Several villagers reclining along the store wall greet me. One of the men introduces his companion as the commandante, assigned to the village by the army. The commandante eyes me with a crooked smile. He's about 35, tall and muscular, with a short military haircut.

I ask one of the men about getting a boat ride upstream to Púcuro, the next village on my excursion. He directs me to another man beside the shack, a tall middle-aged black chap who owns a motor-dugout.

The boat owner speaks a little English. To avoid the hassle of bartering I offer him a decent price up front. "Are you going to Púcuro?" I ask.

"Yes, I go to Púcuro tomorrow."

"You'll take me as a passenger for 20 dollars?"

He reflects for a moment. "Okay," he agrees, "I'll take you. Meet here tomorrow morning at seven."

*   *   *   *

The sidewalk in front of the store seems to be a meeting place; about a dozen people have gathered here to chat. I meet one man who says he is from Púcuro and that he plans to travel back there in a few days. He is a Kuna native who left the rainforest to live in the city. Now he is returning to Darien to convince the locals to elect him in the coming national election to represent them in the capital.

Down by the riverside three men are repeatedly yanking a starter cord to turn over an outboard motor. As the men fidget and yank, the outboard screams to life and they scramble for cover. Then the screaming sputters and dies. In anger the men thrash it with sticks. Then they shove their noses into the engine and resume their fiddling.

A bottle of cola here is twice the price that it was in Panama City, and quadruple the price I remember in Honduras or El Salvador. Maybe I'll buy a bottle later.

Another man starts chatting with me. He tells me that the other expeditioners, my compatriots, stayed here a few days, but they left this morning.

I ask one of the storeside loiterers about a woman named Maria whom I've heard will provide lodging for a traveler. "She's dead," he answers.

*   *   *   *

I wander along the sidewalk to find a place to stay. I approach one man standing in front of his shack and ask him whether he knows a place I can lodge tonight. "Yes," he says, "I can put you up in a place tonight."

"I'll give you two dollars," I offer.

"Two dollars!" he says. "A good place to stay is worth more than two dollars."

"Okay, three dollars."

"I don't know," he says, stroking his beer belly and pondering my offer. "Three dollars is a little low."

He seems like he's about to accept my offer, then the two boatmen who tried to scam me walk over. "Watch out for this one," they warn, trying to support his bartering. "We brought him all the way from Unión de Choco and he paid us only four dollars."

The man looks at me with disgust. "What — only four dollars!" Then he continues. "Five dollars to lodge tonight, no less!"

"Five dollars!" I exclaim. "Five dollars to lodge one night?"

"Yes."

"Alright, I will pay you five dollars," I concede, "but only if you provide me dinner as well."

83

The man meditates a moment. "Very well, five dollars including dinner. Alright, come along then."

I follow him to a faded peach-colored shack. He leads me inside to an empty main room then to the left through a door into a tiny spartan bedroom. Wow, they have a cot to sleep in here! I dump my pack beside the cot and pay him the five dollars. Before he leaves he tells me to meet him at his shack at five o'clock this evening for the dinner.

Most of my cash is in 20-dollar bills. But I find a spare one-dollar bill and decide to visit the supply store to buy a cold soda. I walk back outside, feeling pleasantly unencumbered without my heavy pack. My shack is only a few doors down from the store. I buy a Coke and quickly guzzle it. The Coke tastes so fabulous that I immediately ask for another. No wonder these people think North Americans seem rich, spending a whole dollar on soda pop.

I return to the shack to take a nap. Above my cot is an open window. What a view! — framed between the white windowpanes a luscious jungle soars into the sky, chattering and squawking, drooping great vines that waft in the hot breeze and dangle lazily into the gurgling river.

Tucked in the opposite corner of the room is another cot with an elderly man resting atop a blanket. With all the decades he's spent here in the Darien he probably possesses some phenomenal stories. But now he is old; he seems about 90 years, and very feeble. Maybe he is suffering from a disease, like cancer. His legs are like mere toothpicks wrapped in floppy brown trousers.

Patriotic school posters plaster the opposite wall of the room. In one, boys cheerily sweep the schoolyard, scrub the floors and mend broken desks. In another, a clean, happy school glows vibrantly, backdropped by a multi-colored sun. The posters are not only cheerful, they also block the breeze from blowing through the slits in the wall.

Another poster portrays a fat, smiling "Pedro Politica." One hand is grasping a gun; the other hand is holding a brimming bag of broken promises. Beside Pedro, a collection of newspaper articles covers the wall. The articles discuss bridging Darien with the Pan-American Highway — old articles for an old idea.

Beside my cot the wall is plastered with pages from a 1981 Sears catalog: sewing machines, movie cameras, gum machines, the Proctor Silex Juicer for only $19.99, the Regal Fondue, the Wear Ever (tm) Chicken Bucket, the Northern Hot Dog Steamer, the Rival Ice Crusher. The pages also feature jeans ("the racy look you've seen on TV," ladies bags ("her initials up front") and linens ("your choice — one price buys any fully-quilted bedspread"). The catalog items mean about as much to these villagers as dugout canoes mean to North Americans. Anyone in the village who sees these pages must gape in amazement while envisioning the riches of America.

A young woman enters the room now. She drags a chair over to sit by the old man's bedside. With watery eyes, she gazes at his wrinkled face. He lies there and moans slightly. The day has advanced into early afternoon. A hot breeze blows across the jungle canopy through the open window and tussles the woman's hair. Through the cracks in the wall, slivers of light stripe the old man's slender figure. I lie down to nap. Unmoving, I soon ooze with sweat, but the breeze swishes peacefully through the treetops and I sleep.

*   *   *   *

I wake in mid-afternoon and stare up at my surroundings. The Sears catalog above me stares back. Outside the window the river babbles and the trees tower under the hot blue sky. I sit up. More visitors come to examine the old man. He'll probably give his last groans in the night and at dawn the whole village will crowd into the room to mourn for him.

I left the Hemingway novel back in Unión de Choco. I'm more concerned now with my feet than with the Colonel in Venice. I bend down and examine my soles. I notice a green growth bubbling underneath my blister! I retrieve my razor blade to operate. After carving a pair of slits in a triangle pattern I peel back the skin. Not deep enough. I slice farther but I still don't reach the green. Once again I cut deeper. There. I've sliced down to the green growth. Actually the growth is blackish-green and slimy. I scoop out the slime and spread antibiotic cream into the hole and fold the skin back. With the green eliminated the cut now throbs light red from the blood.

I lie down again, and the old man and I doze for a few more hours. My constant sweating dehydrates me but cleans my pores. A few hours later I wake and rub the sleep from my eyes. A big black man walks into the room. "Speak English?" he asks.

"Yes, do you speak English?" I reply in Spanish.

"No," he answers in Spanish, "but I'm studying it."

The man sits in front of the grandfather, mutters a few words, then glances with curiosity at my belongings and leaves.

I wearily put on my shoes, not bothering to tie them, and I casually wander out to the spot where the banana boats are tied. Reclining on the grass near the supply store, I gaze around at the ragged, multi-colored shacks and imagine the movie you could make about this place — a peculiar and isolated jungle village, the last outpost, the edge of civilization.

Starting tomorrow, my Darien expedition toughens. The riverboat journey in the morning will be my last until Colombia. When the river is high, the boat can motor all the way to Púcuro. But I'm traveling at the end of the dry season. With the river so low, the boat will have to deposit me about half an hour from the village.

After Púcuro, I will spend a full day of arduous bush-hiking to reach the next Kuna village, named Paya. After a further full day of trekking past Paya, if I don't stray off course, I should reach the Colombian frontier. Then begins the second stage of the expedition — the grueling and perilous journey southward from the border to eventually reach Turbo, the seedy Colombian port marking the resumption of the Pan-American Highway.

So far I've inhabited the jungle for four days. Ten days from now I should see road again.

*   *   *   *

When I return to my shack, the old man is beside his cot teetering over a potty. Stepping on his shirt he's on the verge of tipping over. I rush over to help him. His arms are so thin that the elbows jut out like sharp spears. Compared to the few weeks I'll spend in Darien, he has probably lived his whole life here.

After helping the man crawl back into his bed, I ask whether it's true that Colombia is dangerous. He says nothing. But he slowly points at my watch, then raises his hand to his chin and pretends to slit his throat.

I wander back outside to my landlord's shack for dinner. As I pass the store a smiling man approaches me and greets me in English. He says he studied my language for six months at the YMCA in Panama City. We chat about his village. "All the men here are farmers," he explains. "They mostly grow bananas and corn and rice."

The man says he has traveled through every country in Central America and as far north as the Mexico-US border, where smugglers offered to sneak him into America for 1500 dollars.

He also tells me that a Canadian once stayed here for three years. "Before he left for Colombia, the Canadian said he would send me back a message that he reached the other side. But I never heard from him again. I worry that the banditos or guerillas killed him." The man looks at the ground and shakes his head with grief, then he says good evening and walks away.

I continue to my landlord's house. The man offers me a seat by his table. The whole front of his house is open to the breeze — not that you would really need a wall in this tropical cauldron. After a few minutes his wife places in front of me a bowl of rice with a fish on top. I chew happily — by now the occasional pebble in the rice doesn't bother me.

Meanwhile some of the friendly blacks gather by the table and examine my "gringo machete," the one I bought near Yaviza. Even though it's nothing more than a sharpened piece of sheet metal with a plastic handle, my machete fascinates them. When the sly landlord sees it he disappears behind the shack and emerges a second later with his rusty old cutlass. "Look," he says, smiling, "I will trade you my fine machete for your machete." I agree to the swap. I get a short, rusty blade, but with a sleek marble-like handle. He gets my bigger, brand-new machete with a plain black plastic handle. I wanted a smaller one anyway, so we both appreciate the exchange. The man walks out the back door and exhibits his new blade to the other villagers. "Yes," he exclaims proudly. "It's new — isn't it elegant!"

When I finish my meal the woman puts my empty dish on the floor; a dog, a cat and a duck rush over and devour the scraps.

I saunter to the store. The army officer is sitting by the front porch drinking a bottle of rum. Clad in a sleek blue shirt and flashy jeans and shiny black shoes, his only duty seems to be to look tough and fashionable. Beside him stands a warrior-like boy, not more than four years old, naked except for a jaguar-tooth necklace and a spear. I try to photograph the little warrior but he runs off frightened.

I ask an older boy how many people live in this village. He too runs off, but he returns a few seconds later and says, "About 400 to 500."

In a field behind the shacks, the clamorous generator rumbles to life. For the next five hours, from six o'clock to eleven o'clock, the generator will illuminate the few dangling light bulbs, empower the occasional radio, and chill the freezer in the supply store.

After buying some ginger biscuits in the store, I sit on the porch. Some women rush in front of me chasing a rooster that they want to mate with a chicken. But throughout the race the rooster stays a few feet ahead of the chasers. Then he flaps up into a tree.

Once again an exquisite evening sky blushes over the rainforest. Like tufts of flaming cotton candy streaked with deep violet, the cirrus clouds stretch over the endless green canopy far into the horizon.

A soft breeze whips dust off the sidewalk into the Tuira. The villagers emerge from their shacks and meander to the riverside to chat.

Several boys are walking along the sidewalk now, handing out newspapers. One boy hands me a copy. After reading just a few words I discover that the newspaper is actually a political circular. Hey! Smiling back at me from the cover photo is the chief from Unión, brandishing his early-Beatles haircut!

The villagers are sitting by the riverside now reading their free newspapers. Some of the girls are sitting on the grass with cosmetic gadgets to make up their hair. The savage little warrior boy reappears, though now he's wearing underwear and holding a broomstick.

The sun withdraws and the clouds fade from red to gray. As darkness descends I decide that Boca de Cupe seems to be a pleasant little river port: lightbulbs dangle in front of the colorful shacks and reflect off the bubbling river; lively music buzzes from the radio inside the store; and the villagers chase chickens between the shacks. Hearing some strange barks, I turn my head and notice that it's not only chicken mating season, but it's dog-mating season as well. Perhaps this is the romantic time of year in Darien.

*   *   *   *

I stroll along the sidewalk to explore the village. At the end of the pavement I discover two tiny white churches — one Catholic and one Protestant. Beyond that I find a scrawny shack that says "Armed Forces of Panama" — probably just the commandante's abode.

As I walk farther I see a long shack, decorated with Christmas ornaments. The shack resonates with dance music. Wow, it's a little bar! Behind the bar, a concrete school sulks under the giant jungle trees. Beyond the school the jungle creatures giggle and howl, the satin black sky glimmers with stars and the disco tunes drift over the treetops in the soft breeze.

I turn around and wander toward the opposite end of the village. As I approach the path by the banana boats, my slovenly landlord emerges and accosts me. "Can you lend me four dollars?" he asks.

"When will you pay it back? I'm leaving at seven tomorrow morning."

"I promise I'll return it to you first thing in the morning before you leave."

He acts so pitiful that I grudgingly lend him the four dollars. "Tomorrow before seven," I pronounce, "plus a free breakfast."

"Very well. At 6:30 be at the house for breakfast and I will return your money."

As he walks away I stand and think: he probably needs the money either to urgently pay off a debt, or to urgently sit in on a card game. I ponder — if this guy has no money tonight then do I really expect him to have money at seven o'clock tomorrow morning?

I continue walking through the village. The generator at the edge of the field whines in the darkness. The shacks glow with electric lights, while portable stereos moan love songs. I wonder what this peculiar river village looks like from far above the canopy — a sparkle of light and melody embedded in darkness.

At the other end of the village I find another little bar. Inside, a few stools face the counter. I venture in, perch on one of the stools and order a beer. Behind the counter an ancient stereo pounds a fuzzy beat. I'm the lone customer.

As I swig my beer I notice a novel contraption by my feet. Affixed below the entire length of the bar counter is a sloping gutter leading to a hole in the floor. I wonder whether the gutter is a time-saving invention for the patrons — when the bathroom calls after a few beers, the men simply unzip, urinate against the counter, and the urine flows away down the hole.

I contemplate my surroundings. I'm sitting alone in a tiny, filthy saloon in the last outpost of civilization. A mystical river is gurgling just a few yards beyond the door. And a pack of monkeys is yelping in the treetops outside the window.

I pay for my beer and meander back to my shack. Relaxing on their front porches, the villagers greet me. "Hello, Canadian." Word spreads quickly about the village visitor.

I shuffle into my room and glance at the snoozing grandfather. The poor chap — his entire purpose now is to sleep and eat and go to the bathroom.

I sit on my bed. No sheet, no blanket — but to a weary traveler this cot is paradise. I stash my switchblade and flashlight under my pillow, then I lie back and close my eyes.

Latin Americans savor their racket. Music blares in almost every restaurant, bar, shop or bus — and, with its nifty generator, Boca de Cupe is no exception. Latin dance tunes buzz through the village. Funky reggae pounds in the shack next door. Then 11 o'clock arrives. The clamorous generator shuts off. The music dies. The village blackens. The villagers snooze. One of my last thoughts before I drift asleep is that I want to hop in a bathtub and throw my clothes in a washing machine, but I know I wouldn't find either the tub or the washer for a hundred miles.

UPRIVER THROUGH THE WILDS

Dawn breaks over Boca de Cupe. The roosters erupt with spasms of crowing. Slivers of light spear the cracks in the wall and splice the dusty air. On the porch next door, an old man croons a folk song to salute the rising sun.

I sit up and slap my bare feet onto the warm wooden floor. Then I slip into my battered shoes and pack. After saying farewell to the old man, I don my knapsack and march outside.

I'm limping less today. My pack feels light and my new machete feels smooth and secure between my fingers. A pleasant breeze wafts around the shacks. Now an old woman is singing to greet the new day. Her weathered voice caresses the waking village and floats across the quiet jungle canopy. Two men are standing by the banana boats, jabbering about the river. "No, man — she's too dry," one insists.

At my landlord's house the woman gives me coffee and fried bread. When her husband emerges he smiles sheepishly and presents me two dollars and fifty cents. I count it and look up at him. Embarrassed, he says that if I wait a few more minutes he will try to get the rest for me. A few minutes later his young son bounds through the back door panting and holds out his hand to his father. "Yes, I was able to borrow some," he says excitedly.

"How much?" the relieved father asks.

"Ten cents."

"Ten cents?!" He swipes the coin. "Get out of here!" he scolds as he slaps his son. "I need dollars!"

His wife looks at me mournfully. "We're always lacking money in this house. Always."

Seven o'clock arrives. The humiliated landlord drops a few more coins in my hand. A dollar can injure a man's pride when he doesn't have it. I sigh and mutter that I release him from the rest of the debt. He thanks me.

I hoist my pack and walk down to the banana boats. The tall black man from yesterday is loading his dugout. With him are two younger men who look like natives. One of them takes my pack and squeezes it among the rest of the gear.

While they load the dugout I retrieve my toothbrush and wade into the shallows of the river to brush my teeth. The boat owner climbs the muddy bank and wanders beyond the supply store. A few minutes later he returns with two rifles, which he lays carefully in the stern. "Come on," he urges. "Time to go."

We shove the boat off the sandbank and clamber in. One of the natives yanks the outboard to life, which shatters the morning silence, then he lowers the propeller into the still water. We swivel slowly into the current. Sunshine begins to creep over the shaded morning riverbanks as we accelerate upstream. Within seconds we're ripping over the placid waters, whipping up a backspray like the plume of a snowy peacock and slicing through the occasional floating banana leaf.

The boat owner reclines beside his rifles and studies the water ahead. Although barefoot and dirty, he appears too noble to pilot the dugout unless his labor is truly necessary.

In about five hours we should reach Púcuro. Twenty dollars seems so expensive for such a short journey. In Mexico 20 dollars would carry me 800 miles by bus, the whole 20-hour trip from Mexico City to the Guatemalan border.

* * * *

As we skirt around a bend in the river the horizon rises with luxuriant green hills. The occasional hut speckles the shoreline, surrounded by monumental trees.

After about half an hour of traveling we pull ashore beside a narrow trail and a short black man ambles down from a hut to chat with the boat owner. After exchanging pleasantries, the boat owner begins making a lot of business excuses about a job he promised to fulfill for the other man.

Sensing that we might be waiting here for a while, the native at the front of the dugout asks to borrow my machete to sharpen the pole he uses to thrust us around rocks. Meanwhile a family of quacking ducks plods down the footpath to see us, and a ripe mango drops from a tree, bounces off the bank, and splashes into the water.

A sudden shriek from the opposite bank seizes our attention. Two dogs are attacking a pig tied up by the riverside. They savagely tear its face. A man bolts out of a nearby hut, screams at the dogs, and charges down the trail. He grabs a stick and thrashes the fleeing beasts and eventually kicks them into the river. After examining the damaged pig the man clenches his fist, screams, and starts to hurl sticks at the escaping mutts.

An exquisite swan floats by the boat with her babies paddling behind. I look down into the water and notice numerous fish cavorting under the glistening surface.

The men are talking about trust now. "What you did was very damaging," says the short one.

Meanwhile the natives are conversing with each other enthusiastically. Then one of them turns to me and says, "In Canada there are no parties or dances, right?" I assure him that in Canada there are many parties and dances.

The men complete their discussion. We push off the shore and fire up the engine. As we pick up speed the boat owner starts muttering cusses about the man he was talking to.

*　*　*　*

Soon the Tuira narrows and becomes rocky. Seeing rapids ahead, the sternsman revs the outboard and we rip upstream. Then he lifts the prop and we whip through the foamy spray.

More rapids advance toward us. Once again he accelerates then lifts the prop. Bubbling water suddenly encircles us, as though we're boiling in a witch's cauldron. The poler digs into the rocky river bottom and heaves. We inch forward. A few minutes later we emerge from the rapids and the sternsman lowers the prop again.

Another treacherous rapids. Once again giant swirls envelop us, ready to swallow a man as easily as they swallow a dropping leaf. Now both of the natives pole. Tongues hanging out, they wince with pain as the dugout slowly starts drifting backward. A quick dip of the prop by the owner relieves them and propels us upstream.

We skim across the water as the low morning sun peeks and then hides behind the jagged hillsides. Leaving Yaviza, I left the road behind me. Leaving Boca de Cupe, I leave the barest remnants of civilization behind me. I'm now surveying the true wilds of Darien — out here we're far from even the scent of any other human. In fact the only aroma one detects here is a floral fragrance drifting across the river, like you'd find in a fine perfume shop.

The Tuira relaxes into a serene, glassy ribbon. Immense slabs of rock rise along the riverbanks and form a narrow canyon. At the top of the canyon, hundreds of feet above us, monstrous trees lean over to form a twisted ceiling to the canyon. We motor smoothly through the tranquil waters of the tunnel as birds chatter far above on the cliffs.

Now that the river has flattened, the men withdraw hunks of fried bread from their sacks and devour a late breakfast. We peacefully round a corner, then one of the men yells — we duck a hanging branch.

The native lads speak a raucous Spanish that I find hard to understand. But we chat a bit, and occasionally they glance at me writing my notes — they seem to respect that I'm writing about their river.

More rapids appear. We fly into them wildly, then swing over by the shore. With their mouths full of breakfast, the men holler, but skillfully propel us around the rocks. We continue, but a few minutes later we have another round of hollering as we skid over a dry rock peeking up through the water. Each time we fly over a rapids I feel like we're climbing another few feet. And the higher we climb the more treacherous the river becomes. Then in a few more weeks the rains will unleash and transform the river into a raging torrent. Thankfully I'll be long gone by then.

The black man is maneuvering the outboard now. More rapids approach. "Motor!" yell the natives.

"Easy!" returns the pilot. The youths look at me, smiling. They love their river challenge.

The Tuira widens once more. Then I hear a buzzing behind us. Two more dugouts are zooming up the river. Sitting in one boat is a pretty native woman who smiles at the lads. Sitting in the other boat are several native children.

I smell cooking fires and notice the roofs of some huts on a hill by the west shore. The pilot silences the engine. We drift to the opposite shore and stop beside some tall bushes separated by a slender path. Farther up the hillside the trees encircle a sugarcane plot.

"This trail leads to Púcuro," the boat owner says. "It's about two hours walk." But the man speaks hesitantly, as though he's not really sure where the trail goes. We notice a native woman standing on the opposite shore looking at us. "This trail leads to Púcuro, doesn't it?" he shouts across the river.

"Yes," she answers. "It is up that way — the trail is like a highway."

Not wanting to argue (with three of them against one of me) I give him the 20 dollars, even though he agreed yesterday that the fare would take me to a trail that is about 30 minutes from Púcuro.

I climb out of the boat onto the shore. The native boys hand me my pack. I lift it onto my back and carefully climb the steep trail to the top of the bank, about 30 feet above the water. The three men sit sedately in the boat and watch me, fascinated with this gringo venturing alone into the foreboding rainforest, perhaps wondering whether I'll change my mind and ask to come back into the safety of the dugout. They wait until I reach the top of the bank and disappear into some bushes. Then I hear the boat gurgle to life and they push away from the shore and they're saying something about "the gringo" and laughing and the gurgling motor fades into the distance and I hear only the swishing of the shrubs in the sultry breeze.

I sit at the top of the bushy riverbank and check my map. From up here I can see the native village across the river. I don't know its name or its tribe, and it's not marked on the map. But I don't want to dwell on such matters — I want to start trekking to Púcuro.

My watch reads 9:30 a.m. — still a few more hours until the oppressive midday heat. Pleasant aromas from the village's cooking fires drift across the water. A few feet farther up the trail a rhythmic machete chopping echoes through the treetops.

I stand up and begin hiking up the path. After I walk a few dozen feet the trees clear and I emerge on the edge of a banana tree plot. The villagers have recently harvested the fruit, and they've burned the field to fertilize it for the next crop. I stop walking. Although the day is early the sun is already scorching the blackened field. Waves of heat waft upwards. As I stand in the shade grimacing at the baking field the sun disappears behind a cloud. I dash along the path and reach the shade on the other side just before the sun reappears.

I continue along the trail. But after walking just a few more feet I hear sounds — footsteps are following me. After cautiously turning my head I notice a native boy with his pet dog. I stop and sit beside the path. Slowly and shyly the boy walks over and sits near me. "Hola," I say.

"Hola," he answers.

I say nothing for a few moments. He watches me. "So how is the way to Púcuro?" I ask.

"The trail is good," he replies. "You will reach Púcuro in about three hours."

I ask him how many gringos come through here every year. "About ten per year," he reckons. "But yesterday five gringos passed through here at once."

"Ah, yes. They are acquaintances of mine."

The boy is chewing a stick of sugarcane. He balances the cane on his neck so he can eat without using his hands (much like we balance telephones on our necks in North America to busily scribble a message). He sucks out the sugar juice and spits away the bad bits. (And they say North American kids are addicted to sugar?) After a while he breaks off a chunk and offers it to me.

The dog rolls playfully in the dirt. "How old is he?" I ask.

"He has eight months now."

I blow my nose. By this stage in my Darien travels I have forsaken handkerchiefs. I simply blow into my hand then wipe my palm in my shirt. Having done this for a few days, however, my shirt has become crusted with mucous. But maybe if I wash it well it will show that stylish worn-in look.

"Do you know what day it is?" I ask the boy (to see whether his tribe keeps time as the outside world.)

"Yes, it is Monday."

"How many families live in your village?"

"About 60."

"And how many siblings have you?"

Like many children I've met in Latin America, he has to think for a moment before answering that question. "Only four," he finally concludes. "I'm the eldest — I have 14 years."

I now realize that the riverboat owner ripped me off this morning. The boat journey to Púcuro takes five or six hours. He only ferried me two hours upstream. He never intended to carry me close to Púcuro, but he grabbed the opportunity to swipe my 20 dollars.

I gaze toward the distant western mountains. "How long is it to walk there?"

He looks at them and laughs. "Quién sabe?" he says. "Who knows? There is nobody over there."

He throws the dog a chunk of cane. The dog knows how to peel the skin and eat the sweet inside, but he has to pause to roll in the dirt to scratch his fleas. Then his ears perk and his eyes widen and he leaps away to chase a lizard. The boy and I relax on the cool breezy trail and I ask if he has a woman or a wife yet and we laugh a little.

"Can I see your arm," I ask. He shows me, and I notice vaccination marks.

I ask him whether many pumas roam these parts. "Yes, there are many black cats on the trail to Púcuro, and many serpents and boas that are very dangerous."

I ask him whether his people eat the snakes. "Of course we don't — only the pumas eat the snakes."

Then I ask him about the social customs in his village. "Do the men take only one wife?"

"Most have only one wife," he tells me. "But not my uncle," he adds.

"Are there many women that have children but don't have husbands?"

"Yes, many. And we also have many people who don't own shoes."

"What religion have you?"

"We have no religion in my village. Only a few have books. So most don't believe."

"Do you believe in God?"

"Yes, I believe, but only a few of us in the village believe."

I decide that I'm thinking too much and resting too much and chatting too much and that I should start trekking. I stand. "Will I meet any others on the trail?"

"No, only you and the cats will be using the trail."

Suddenly we hear a heavy shuffling amidst the bushes. We both glance toward the sound. The shuffling stops. My neck hairs quiver. My eyes meet the boy's eyes and we both wonder, but say nothing. I stand up and say farewell. He rambles down the trail back to the village. I begin trekking up the cavernous path.

*   *   *   *

Like a mystical tunnel the spindly path winds through dense bush, laboriously ascending, as though leading to a dark, wicked castle. At any moment, I fret, one of the plump mossy limbs might swoop down — a monstrous, starving boa eager for a feast.

Every few seconds horrendous roots snag my feet. Every few minutes walls of cobwebs block the path. My footsteps and my scent travel ahead of me, forewarning my arrival to any beasts on the trail ahead. As I penetrate deeper into the bowels of Darien the only companions with me are the droning bees, the fluttering scarlet butterflies, the occasional lizard scampering across the trail and the endless columns of ants.

The trail crests a hill and reaches a plateau. I pause to rest at this modest summit. The foliage up here is more open. My elevated vista reveals a stunning panorama of the jungle below, stretching for miles, a green carpet rising and dipping and stretching to the horizon. I imagine all the thousands of beasts beneath that canopy, snorting and slurping and stalking.

As I sit on the trail beside a termite-infested log, glistening green caterpillars fall from the sky onto my forearms. I brush them off and stare bewildered at the hundreds of insects covering every foot of the forest floor. I stand up. The ground is too alive for my taste. Only after standing do I realize that I was resting my back against a mammoth dead tree, its topmost branches towering naked in the heavens, its hollowed heart roomy enough to harbor a family of natives, or a family of pumas.

Midday is approaching. A few clouds float across the light-blue sky. The hot wind swirls through the treetops. Though I'm sore and soaking with sweat and dreading the endless and punishing hike ahead, my adventure across the Gap exhilarates me.

A few feet beyond my resting spot the trail forks. I take a compass reading. I reckon I should follow the path on the left, but I'm not sure. I drop my pack. Carrying only the machete and compass, I venture to scout the trail. After exploring just a few hundred feet I conclude that this is the correct route. I retrieve my pack and resume trekking.

The path twists around tree trunks the width of elephant bellies and vines the width of elephant legs. Termites and rot have completely hollowed some of the trees into spacious dens. I stumble across a highway of ants that are crossing the trail carrying morsels of fruit. So frequently traveled is their path that they've worn a groove through the soil.

The hiking becomes an arduous monotony: continually pushing forward, one foot in front of the other. As far as I know I'm venturing through a no-man's-land between the lands of the Choco and Kuna tribes, who are longstanding enemies.

Suddenly two birds flap out from some bushes beside the trail and screech up to the treetops. I pause once more to rest. Noises surround me — from small animals scurrying across the floor to the frequent crash of overripe mangoes dropping from the treetops.

I stand up and push on. Midday passes. For a few more miles the trail climbs, then it suddenly dips and I descend a path that I see no end to — down, down, down, into hot misty shadows. Then I hear a sound behind me. I stop. Something is following me. Something big. I quicken my pace. After a few heart-rending moments the sound tapers and disappears.

*　　*　　*　　*

As I hike farther the bush becomes denser. Now only the barest slivers of sunlight penetrate to the ground. I sit down and consult my compass again.

"Why does it keep reading north-northeast?" I curse. According to my map the trail should go south-southeast, not north-northeast. As I ponder the bearing on my compass I feel a whack on the back of my head. Stunned, I look beside me. It was just a clump of ripe berries. I look up. The wind still whips through the canopy far above, but down here in the murky depths the air lies still.

I check my feet to examine the blister that I operated on in Boca de Cupe. The wound is still clean, and I'm limping less. If the wound worsens, or if any illness or injury befalls me here, I'm alone and my remaining days might be few. I decide to get up and continue walking even though a fascinating toad is hopping beside my pack.

The trail follows a ridge with the terrain sloping ever so slightly at each side. Then it dips once more. Every few minutes I think I see a sunny clearing ahead, perhaps a field signaling Púcuro. But every time the clearings turn out to be the sun glinting off a spread of bushes on the lower ground ahead — just a mirage.

When I reach the bottom of the dip I discover a creek bed, dry as a desert. As I shuffle my feet in the arid dirt a screech shatters the silence in front of me. As I raise my machete an enormous stork-like bird lifts into the air.

I push on, but a few minutes later the trail expires. I stare into a wall of vines and bushes and lament. "Now where do I go?"

I drop my pack and begin scouting. Somewhere in front of me the trail must resume. But a few dozen feet beyond my backpack I have to stop walking: the foliage is impenetrable. I peer through the leaves to scan the thickets ahead — just olive-colored bushes and more bushes and more bushes and then my eyes glimpse a large black outline rustling behind one of the bushes. "What is that!" Heart racing, I disentangle myself from the vines and sprint back to the open area by my pack — if that thing is going to attack me then I want to be in the open, not trapped in a bush. "That was a puma!" says my racing mind. "It must have been. It was big and black — that must have been a puma!"

I catch my breath for a few minutes, then I cautiously stalk around the bushes, listening to every rustle, peering intently. The beast has disappeared. But at least I find the trail again. I return for my bag and struggle around the thicket and set off again, nervously glancing over my shoulder. Perhaps it was just a wild boar.

*   *   *   *

My pack is so weighty that it restricts my circulation. I remember when I first stuffed this knapsack in Canada a few days before I left for Latin America. I proudly hoisted the olive green bag onto my back and strutted through the house. After traipsing around the kitchen for a few minutes I decided that even though the pack was heavy I could handle it. But I soon discovered that walking around my parents' kitchen is far different than walking mile after mile along the streets and trails of Central America. Just a few hours after landing in Mexico I fathomed my plight. I found that I could walk only a few minutes before the unbearable weight of the pack compelled me to rest. In fact for every five minutes I walked I had to devote ten minutes to rest. Over the next days and weeks and months I gradually relieved myself of superfluous belongings and reduced the knapsack to a more manageable weight. Nonetheless, three months and seven countries later the pack is still a ponderous hulk.

The spindly trail continues to wind and dip and climb. The steep ascents, each about 50 feet long, hinder me the most. Each time I surmount a hill I ease my knapsack and my panting body to the ground to rest. I lay my head down, using the pack as a pillow, and I close my eyes. Each time I rest I'm almost sure I hear distant voices, but then I'm not sure they are voices, and in the end I'm not sure that I heard anything at all.

No sign of Púcuro, though I should have reached it hours ago. Even worse, the trail continues to wander farther from the proper course. For the first few hours I didn't worry about the direction of the path. I reckoned it would eventually veer onto the bearing indicated on my scrappy map. But ever since morning the trail has run about 60 degrees off the proper bearing. I also haven't encountered a river that I was supposed to cross hours ago. Now I'm becoming weary and dehydrated. No village is in sight. Deep in this hot, misty jungle I realize that I don't know where I am.

BANANAS

I walk around to stretch my tired back and to think. I find some plump brown vines and decide to swing on one, so that I'll one day remember when I traveled solo through the jungle, swinging on vines like Tarzan. I rush forward and leap onto one of the mossy ropes, but the stiff vine doesn't swing like a rope at all.

Out of curiosity I wander about a hundred feet off the trail to glimpse a spot of jungle untouched by any human. I find nothing interesting; or at least nothing interesting enough to keep me from returning to my pack and resuming my search for this native village.

Since I've come this far I'll continue along this route. This trail must lead to something — hopefully soon. I lift my pack and resume trudging along the narrow corridor. Though monotonous, the walking no longer bothers me — except for the occasional laborious hill.

Suddenly a colorful scrap seizes my attention — a package of Lucky Strike cigarettes. The discarded box lies crumpled and faded on the side of the trail against a plump red tree. It might have rested here for years, perhaps even from as far back as the British Army expedition in 1972.

I continue walking, but after a few more minutes I stop to rest once more. My hair is matted with sweat and my heart is pounding madly. I glance up at the cracks of blue sky. Far above me a long-armed monkey is leaping through the air between branches.

I push onward. Within a few minutes I discover another creek. Dry. A few minutes farther I find another dry creek, then another. I suppose these are good signs. My water is low. If I deplete my supply I can follow a dry streambed down to a river.

*   *   *   *

The terrain transforms. The path begins to run flat now. The dirt becomes soft and black and the air smells moist and earthy. Sweeping ferns surround me. Stubby trees bulge with giant bean pods.

I stop to listen. Is that a river or wind? No, it's just the wind. I check the compass. The trail has veered even farther off course.

Five hours from the start of my trek the jungle transforms further. The trees push apart. The floor blackens more and a peat fragrance floods my nostrils. Peculiar squawks and moans echo around me. As I walk onward the ruckus intensifies.

High above the trail, tiny monkeys scurry from tree to tree and dozens of birds flutter from branch to branch. As I hasten through the ruckus I remain hopeful that I'll emerge somewhere useful at the end of this trail, maybe even before nightfall; but I'm beginning to doubt that the somewhere will turn out to be Púcuro.

A few miles farther I spot another shred of civilization — a piece of plastic cookie wrapper. The trail begins to steadily ascend. Eventually it plateaus and widens. Is that a banana tree? Yes, it's a lone banana tree beside the trail. A few minutes later I discover another banana tree, and another and another. The trail widens even more. Now banana trees surround me. I smell smoke. I hear voices ahead. Then the trail dips. Brilliant sun strikes my face. I stand on the edge of a meadow. On its opposite edge stands a concrete shack, probably another jungle school. Beyond the shack the grassy heath turns to dirt, topped by dozens of wooden huts.

I stroll across the field to the nearest hut. As I approach its side I notice two men sitting on a bench. Hey, that's the guy from Boca de Cupe — the one running for the National Assembly. I approach him and say hello. He shakes my hand. "What village is this?" I ask.

"This is Púcuro," he says. Then he turns to his compatriot, a chubby, grouchy-looking man of about 25 years, whom he introduces as the chief. I ask the chief if I may stay in his village for a few days. He grumpily assents.

As I wander between the huts, looking for a spot to erect my hammock, I come across an astonishing sight — a shack built with wooden planks, lined with screened windows, boasting a table and chairs inside, and a white woman standing by the door dressed like a North American. "Hola," I say hesitantly.

"Hola," she responds.

"Are you a traveler?" I ask in Spanish.

"No, I live here with my husband. We are missionaries," she answers.

"Where are you from?"

"The United States — from Florida," she continues in Spanish.

"Ahh. So I guess you speak English then."

"Yes," she answers, now in English. "Would you like a glass of water?"

"Yes. Thank you."

She walks into the house and returns a moment later with the glass. "So you are a traveler?" she asks.

"Yes. I plan to stay here just a few days. Then on to Colombia."

"Well, I hope you have a good journey," she says as she walks back into the house. Then she adds, "I think you have to go to that big hut in the center of the village and show the man there your passport. He records it in a book."

I glance at my watch. After enduring six and a half hours of blistering hiking (without even knowing whether the trail would lead to Púcuro) it is now late afternoon.

I saunter toward the big hut in the center of the village. Constructed of sticks, the spacious hut would comfortably shelter at least two large families. I approach one of the doorways and notice a chubby middle-aged native inside swaying in a hammock. The man greets me and tells me that two Swedes stayed in the village yesterday. He asks for my passport and tells me to return later to pick it up.

With the villagers gazing at me, I traipse around to find some tree trunks to support my hammock.

*   *   *   *

The men here wear baggy pants and loose shirts. Anthropologists say the Kuna men adopted their current style of dress half a millennium ago from the European explorers to the New World.

The women wear multi-colored skirts and blouses of scarlet, violet and yellow, meticulously embroidered with elaborate designs. Some women exhibit dozens of colorful, beaded necklaces. Others display delicate gold nose rings or thick gold bracelets and anklets.

Sleek black hair crowns the heads of all the tanned and barefoot villagers; flowing long on the women, chopped short on the men. Within a few seconds I perceive that these are truly different people to the Choco that I stayed with previously — their homes, their appearance, their mannerisms, their language, their attitudes. One of their few similarities is their common food — bananas, rice, fish and sometimes a little bush meat like wild boar.

Most of the huts are little one-room rectangles, built with flimsy bamboo walls and arched roofs of banana leaves. The village lies atop a brown dirt field, about 20 huts arranged in three rows. The huts are bordered on the north by the expansive green meadow beneath the end of the trail, on the east by sweeping fields of banana trees and sugarcane, and on the west by a forest of slender palm trees. When I stroll to the south end of the village, behind one row of huts and beyond some bushes, I discover the shallow Púcuro River, gurgling faithfully under the blistering sun of the high-dry season.

A troop of shy children shuffles toward me to examine the tall and ragged white man. But, noticing the machete clasped in my hand, they dash away frightened to scrutinize me from afar.

I find some poles beside an abandoned shack alongside the river. After relieving myself of my heavy pack, I realize that I've dropped the prized hunting knife that I carry in my belt. The sheath hangs empty.. "Man, where did I drop that?" I fret. I examine the ground around me. Nothing but beige earth. Oh well, I still have my machete for the bush and my switchblade for the cities.

I pull out my hammock and string it to the poles. Then I retrieve my canteen and wander down to the river to fill it with water. As I traipse along the short, parched trail to the shoreline I notice that the river is only about 30 feet wide. In fact you wouldn't perceive the river if you were scanning the landscape from just a few dozen feet away; only when you approach the shore do you even realize the Púcuro is here.

I return to the spacious hut in the center of the village to reclaim my passport. The man is still reclining in the hammock, though he's now reading a colorful children's book. After asking me whether I have any Canadian money, to which I reply no, he hands over my passport.

I stroll back to my hammock. Just as I reach it some women beside a hut call out to me. "Do you have any medicines?"

"No, I don't," I holler back.

"Do you have any onions?"

"None."

I walk over to the women. One of them points to a boy, about four years old, sitting beside them. "My son. He is ill."

I suspect that the boy suffers from vitamin-A deficiency, one of the most common childhood ailments in the third world. "I think he needs vitamin-

115

A," I tell her. "Feed him lots of avocados and meat. I think that will help him."

Since I'm already talking to the women, I ask whether they can prepare a meal for me later on. At first they ask me for money, but we barter for a few minutes and they eventually agree to make me some food if I give them a bag of oatmeal.

I return to my hammock to rest, but before I climb into it I notice a slim, bare-chested man returning from the fields and walking to the hut with the two women. After setting down his machete he reclines in a chair to observe me. Soon he calls out to me. "Over here. Bring your hammock over here," he says, gesturing to a pair of poles under a canopy attached to the hut. I untie the hammock and erect it under the overhang beside his home. Extending from the shack, the overhang is an arrangement of sticks supporting a roof of packed leaves. Here the family can prepare their meals over a fire, sheltered from the summer rains.

I introduce myself to the man. He says his name is Luis. I thank him for the shelter. He trudges away to tend to some chores.

I browse around the village some more, and casually wander over to the missionaries' home where I see the minister beside his shack. He appears clean and neat, dressed in shorts and a t-shirt. "Oh," he says as he sees me. "You must be Andrew. My wife told me about you. I'm Rick."

We chat about the village a bit, then he tells me about his mission to evangelize the Kuna here. "Well, it looks like you've got a nice little house while you're here," I remark.

"Yup," he says proudly. "We've got a water purifier, a stove, some sinks, even a refrigerator. Yeah, we've got all the basic facilities."

He goes on to tell me that during the rainy season you can ferry equipment to here via the rivers all the way from the ocean. He also says that every month a plane parachutes in supplies for them.

By the time I drift back to my hut the woman is cooking some oatmeal for me. She seems about 35, and wears more gold than the other villagers. She also seems unfriendly. In fact most of the Kuna here have cast wary glances toward me. Only a few have smiled or greeted me.

The woman places a bowl of the oatmeal atop a rickety wooden table under the canopy. I sit at the table and eat peacefully. I feel happy that I reached my destination, though I'm still bewildered at the puzzling direction of the path today and the length of the journey — six hours instead of two.

* * * *

The heat of the day dissipates and an evening breeze embraces the village. I examine my new home for the next few days. Children frolic around the hut as the late afternoon shadows stretch across the dirt. A few feet from the edge of the shelter the dirt nurtures a growth of bushes and stubby trees. A few dozen feet farther the Rio Púcuro babbles over the rocks.

As I shuffle over to my hammock to rest, a door opens on a nearby shack. Luis and Rick exit with their Bibles, beam at the sky and cry "Alleluia!" I infer that they and the other few leaving the shack have just experienced a satisfying prayer meeting. Luis and the missionary glance at me and begin jabbering in the Kuna dialect and chuckling.

The two stroll over and sit under the shelter. A few minutes later the election candidate emerges and presents Luis with a campaign poster. Unlike the other villagers, the candidate wears jeans and shoes. I ask him about his current occupation. He tells me that he's a newspaper reporter in Panama City, but that he will be the next representative for this area in the National Assembly. "My socialist party and I are very popular here," he professes.

I climb from my hammock and stroll around the village a bit more, thrilled with the blessing of being able to peruse without my burdensome pack. When I return once more to the hut, Luis is holding up the campaign poster and staring at it dreamily, musing over the ideals of socialism. "Fairness for all people..." he extols. "Plenty of money for my family...."

I ask Luis about the village. "We have rice, corn, bananas and sugar," he begins. "We all have our land; there is no shortage. Also, everyone here can read and write."

As we chat about the village I perceive more and more that the natives of this rainforest refer to Panama and Darien separately, as if Darien is semi-sovereign, a vast land independent from the rest of the nation, indeed from the rest of the world.

I borrow a blade file from Luis and sit under the shelter to sharpen my machete. As I'm delicately honing, a monstrous rooster struts toward me from behind the hut, scaring off all the ducks and chickens in his path. The prodigious bird looks like the cartoon character Foghorn Leghorn. I eventually stroke the machete sharp as a razor, though I nick my knuckle.

Evening approaches. The women revive the cooking fires to prepare dinner. Luis reclines in his tattered chair. I ask him more about the village.

"We have about 280 people here," he says. "Most have become evangelicals. A few are Catholic — on Sundays they motor downriver to Boca de Cupe for Mass."

Several women wander over to us and offer to sell me "molas," the embroidered patches decorating their blouses. I decide that the molas would make novel gifts for my family back in Canada. I barter them down from a dream price of 30 dollars to a slab of salami and tin of sardines I bought in San José. The salami and sardines intrigue them because they came from Costa Rica, a faraway land they've only heard about.

After trading for the molas, word gets around and more villagers arrive to barter. As the children swing in my hammock, a half-dozen women examine my provisions. Meanwhile Luis scrutinizes my compass. I explain how it works. "Very valuable," he remarks. "With this you can surely find your way in the jungle." Then, indicating one of his people's superstitious fears, he adds, "Without it you would fall into the ocean."

I try to trade some cheap colorful cigarette lighters, which I bought for this very purpose of bartering, but the canned beans attract the most attention.

When night arrives the traders retire to their homes. Luis seems to have three sons, between the ages of about 10 and 14. Together we sit around the rickety table under the shelter. I light a stubby candle that I bought in Guatemala and place it in the middle of the table.

The eldest son tells me he attends high school with many other natives in El Real, a large village about one day downriver near Unión de Choco. With slicked hair and an arrogant sneer he has returned to Púcuro during school vacations.

"Here, look at my watch," the little huckster proudly urges, showing me a cheap digital. "I will sell it to you for seven dollars."

I decline. Then he holds up the socialist poster. "Ten dollars for this," he offers, then barks immediately, "and tell me how you say candle in Italian."

Bewildered at his curious question I respond that I'm from Canada, not Italy. I conclude that the children of Púcuro have swiftly lost any shyness toward me. Their belligerence contrasts with the polite and friendly temperament of the youth in Unión de Choco.

The boys quarrel over who can try the hammock. After shoving the others away, one skinny lad jumps in and immediately sinks down like a dead fish in a net.

In another attempt to siphon money from me, "Slick" offers to be my guide to Paya, my next destination, for 20 dollars. Once again I decline. Then he tells me that when he first saw me today he thought I was a Colombian, not a gringo.

Now Papa Luis is swinging in the hammock. His wife and daughter are laboring by the fire, preparing to serve our dinner. "We have meat tonight," Luis boasts. "And tomorrow we have stew."

The women present us with plates of meat and boiled bananas. For some reason I assume I'm eating beef. But after finishing my food I recall that I've seen no cows in Darien, so I probably dined on monkey or puma or wild boar.

Most of the annoying children have retreated home for their own dinners. The family and I remain around the table, talking about world economics and about places I've visited, like Mexico City. I determine that they know little about world economics, but they know much about swinging wildly in my precious lightweight hammock to test what altitude they might reach.

As we chat about the countries that I've visited, I begin to understand an amusing misnomer that these natives believe. The family thinks that travelers like me have a boss. They think that traveling is a profession, like dentistry for example, that earns a hefty salary. I explain that to travel you must work at a job, and then use your savings from that job to pay for your journey. They ogle me warily, pondering whether my explanation is a fib.

The conversation drifts onto the destinations I'll encounter on the rest of my Darien journey. Luis tells me he's heard about many rebel groups terrorizing Colombia with names like FARC, ELN and of course the renowned M-19.

The time drifts past nine o'clock. A lethargy overtakes me and implores me to floss and brush my teeth and slip into a deep sleep in my hammock. One by one the weary family members mutter good night and wander inside. Soon only the family's mongrel and

I remain outside in the darkness. The village gradually settles into a deep slumber. After staking my machete in the dirt beside me, I climb into my hammock, sweaty and fatigued.

*   *   *   *

So far I've meandered through Darien for five days — three in Unión de Choco, one in Boca de Cupe and one here in Púcuro. I've already lodged with each of the three peoples inhabiting the Darien — the Choco (or Emberá), the Afro-Panamanians (or Afro-Dariens, as some people call them) and now the Kuna (or Cuna). The rainforest inhabitants have proven to be as fascinating as the rainforest itself.

My next destination is Paya, the ancient capital of the Kuna kingdom, in deepest isolation, about a full day's rugged hiking from here.

After Paya the trek becomes even more grueling. The punishing trail rises through highlands for a full day, peaking at the Colombian frontier. Then the path descends another full day through the Katios National Park to a remote riverside ranger station. According to the natives, I must watch for bandits and rebels once I cross the frontier into Colombia.

Once I make it to the ranger station the trail ends. From there to the first road I must journey by riverboats between several isolated villages. After about a day of motoring I should reach the Great Atrato Swamp, and shortly afterward the broad Atrato River (commonly called "cocaine highway.") After motoring down to the mouth of the Atrato River and across the Gulf of Urabá I will arrive triumphantly in Turbo, the sleazy smugglers cove and the resumption of road.

The dugout canoe journeys from the Katios ranger station to Turbo should take between two and five days, depending on how long I have to wait to find boats traveling downriver.

So a hot bath and a cold beer are still over a week away.

*   *   *   *

I float into slumber, dreaming about roads and buses and restaurants and big cosmopolitan cities, as the jungle clamors and moans around me in quadraphonic stereo.

I wake in the cold of the night suffering terrible stomach pains. My mind sluggishly conjures images of strange dinner meat and dirty river water. I climb from the hammock and hover over a lone red coal dwindling in the fire, then I put on all my clothes, cover my face with my towel and try to rest, clasping my sore gut. Wondering whether malaria has struck me, I wait for the high fever and chills and the joint pains and headaches. But eventually I fall asleep, shivering in the darkness.

After about 3:30 a.m. the jungle clamor fades, except for the thuds of falling coconuts. Spiders drop from the grass-roofed shelter onto my face. Swaying in the cool air I keep my mouth closed as I sleep.

THUNDERCLAPS

Dawn arrives over Púcuro, pale gray at first, then gradually warming into misty orange. The villagers rise in their shacks and walk outside and down to the river to bathe.

The woman of my house emerges and lights the fire, which smokes me out of my hammock. Then she rinses a pot and tosses the water onto the ground. A crowd of ducks frantically flocks to the puddle, slurping the liquid scraps into their beaks, then tilting their heads back and letting the meager nourishment dribble down their throats. One lame duck flaps over and nips seeds from the ground around the woman's feet.

I stroll down to the river with my camera. A half-dozen villagers are crouching in midstream scrubbing themselves and drinking the water. A few dozen feet upstream from the bathers, a woman squats in the river and relieves herself. Doing that downstream would be more hygienic, I think, as I watch the other bathers wash and drink river water a few feet down from her.

When I return to the shack, Luis is cutting firewood, his muscles flexing as he chops into the hard jungle logs. Seeing one of the children husking corn, Foghorn struts over and joins the other animals under the shelter to wait for a morsel. Never have I seen such peaceable mingling of dogs, cats and fowl.

My nighttime sickness symptoms have subsided, aside from a slight aching belly. I delve into my medicine packet for two antacid tablets. Then I take out my shaving cream and toothpaste. The village children arrive to study me. The shaving perplexes them, which is understandable since the Kuna don't grow much facial hair (although Luis sprouts a few black wisps from his chin.)

Beside the fire the family is reading the sardines label. They'll probably treasure it for years. Since they derive all their food directly from the jungle and their fields, any processed food enlivens their life.

The man that looked at my passport yesterday comes to visit. He admires the machete I got from the gambler in Boca de Cupe. "Mmm, very sharp," he says as he draws his thumb across the blade. Then he studies my hammock with fascination. (It always captivates attention). He gingerly sits in it, but he doesn't go so far as to lift his feet off the ground, probably because it's so thin that he's afraid he will puncture it.

My watch reads 7:30. Bright morning light is illuminating the jungle. The women give us breakfast — each male receives three boiled bananas, an egg and watery tea. Even though the females receive no egg, the Kuna women actually have many social rights and a voice in managing their communities. (At this moment they are using their voices to yell at the village's children.)

Slick and his brothers finish their meal and carry a spear down to the river to fish. Throughout the village, men start walking to the fields.

As the morning heat intensifies, the village becomes tranquil. My stomach pains ease. Since I sleep better in the sweaty quiet of the day, I return to the hammock to nap.

My nap lasts from eight until ten. When I wake I know I've slept well because my mouth exudes that fuzzy morning-breath feeling. I open my eyes and see the mother of the house standing by the fire stirring a steaming cauldron.

"What are you making in there?" I ask.

"Corn beer."

As I recline, pondering what I should do today, a girl approaches and offers to sell me some bananas for 15 cents each. It seems that Púcuro's villagers will go to great lengths to snatch my meager monies, considering that bananas grow freely and abundantly around here.

As I sway lazily, I notice a man emerging from one of the jungle trails. On one shoulder he supports a rifle; on the other shoulder he supports a limp wild boar. Meat would make a tasty meal, but I'm actually hoping for fresh fish for lunch.

I stand up and wander over to a nearby trail leading into a field. Beside the entrance to the trail, several women are manipulating a sugarcane press made of logs and sticks.

One woman pushes the cane between the two rollers. Two others jump up and down pulling handles on the edge of each log, which pulls the cane in between the tight rollers. The crushed cane oozes ultra-sweet syrup that dribbles through a funnel made of leaves and down into a bucket. A baby boy chews the shreds of used cane and watches the bucket fill. Everyone will drink the juice later.

The woman feeding the cane through the rollers has limbs adorned with thick gold bands. First put on when she was a child, the bands now painfully constrict her growing legs and arms.

Midday arrives. The village relaxes — a little work, a little chat, a little sweat from the beating sun. I join the Kuna in small talk. As in all the other villages in Darien, the people often ask me whether I still have a father and mother.

As I meander around the huts, I spy a knife hanging on a tree that looks like the one I lost. I walk closer to investigate. A man beside a hut sees me observing the blade and approaches. "May I see your knife?" I ask.

"Yes," he says proudly, and hands it to me readily. "It cost me seven dollars." The sturdy wood-handled hunting knife looks almost identical to my lost one, but different enough that I know it is his.

"Thank you," I say. "It is a very good knife."

*   *   *   *

As the heat of the day climaxes, the dogs lie panting in the dust and the men return from the fields. Sensing that lunch will soon start, Foghorn struts toward the cooking fire to wait for scraps. Just as Luis said last night, we're eating stew today for our midday meal. One of the girls ladles me my lunch, a grand sludge of yams and wild boar. We sit around the table. The family occasionally glances at me, then chatters a few phrases among themselves in their native tongue, then glances at me again. Although they're speaking a different language, I know they're speaking about me.

The suffocating heat of Darien sinks the jungle residents into lethargy. I stare at some husks of corn scattered in the dust and dread tomorrow's punishing hike to Paya, the last village before the Colombian frontier.

The grouchy mother calls out to me. "Can you take care of the house while I go up to the hills for a little bit?" I happily consent, and retreat to my hammock under the shelter to guard the shack and take an afternoon snooze. I close my eyes and swing peacefully from side to side. The thin nylon strands reassuringly support my bare neck. As I drift asleep, my head wobbles from side to side as I sway. Slashes of sunlight flit through the shelter across my face as I swish peacefully through the thick air. A hot breeze strokes the treetops, and every few minutes a coconut drops from a rustling tree and plops into the nearby dust.

Soon the bustle of excited children wakes me: Slick is returning victoriously from the river. His brother follows, lugging a cord holding about 20 shiny black fish. The boys slump onto the bench by the table. Their sister takes the fish and hands each of them a glass of fruit drink. Then she serves them bowls of stew. My mind, however, is craving those delicious fish we'll eat tonight. Food and rest are so vital in this rainforest. Indeed the greatest joys of my life here in Darien are eating and sleeping.

Mama returns now, fresh and clean from bathing by the river. She immediately delves her finger into a tin box and smears colors around her cheeks and eyes while peering into a cracked piece of glass.

Luis reappears. He and the children walk into the house. A few minutes later they emerge, clothed from head to toe with shirts and trousers. "Andrés," he calls out to me. "Can you stay and watch the house while we go to a meeting?"

"Of course," I reply. "What kind of meeting is it?"

"Oh, it's a meeting of the community called by the chief."

I would love to go to this village meeting, but Luis wants me to stay and watch the house. Besides, they likely wouldn't welcome me.

The family struts off together in their best clothes with Mama's face smudged with colors and Luis occasionally skipping as he strives not to catch his bare toes in his long pant cuffs.

After they've disappeared, I peer at the entrance to the shack. I wonder what the inside is like? My curiosity entices me. I scan the silent village. Everyone has gone to the meeting. I wander cautiously to the door, nudge it gently, and peek inside.

Aside from some machetes lying on the dirt floor, the room is barren. Sunlight pierces the cracked boards and streaks the dusty air. Several shelves line the opposite wall. To my right stands a heavy ladder leading to an upper floor.

The second story features a sturdy floor of wooden boards. A partition forms two rooms. Several wide planks lie in each room, covered with blankets for sleeping. Mosquito nets hang around these rigid beds. At the top of the ladder a shotgun rests against the wall. The floor reveals gaping cracks in some areas, but these people are affluent for a native family in the middle of the jungle.

The village still lies quiet while the villagers attend the political assembly. As I lounge in the hammock I decide to examine my feet. My blisters are healing. Noticing that I have a pen in my pocket, I take it and write on my bare sole "You'll make it!" (When I arrive in Turbo my ambition is to wash my clothes and buy fresh socks.)

The family returns from the meeting. Luis immediately strips his uncomfortable shirt and sits in his chair, turning his head to cast a sinister glance at Foghorn, who is scrounging the ground nearby. He reaches over and picks up a sparkling new PALA t-shirt from the candidate to adore it. Then he stands and strips off his troubling pants to reveal against his bronzed body a ratty pair of bland green underwear full of holes.

One of the children fetches the family's archaic radio. A distant melody buzzes by England's Pet Shop Boys. Who knows where the faint signal originates? Panama City? Northern Colombia?

The PALA representative comes to visit me. I ask him about the politics in the country. He explains that the Acción Nacionalista party holds power, and that PRD is to the left, like PALA. If he wins the election he says he will spend most of his time in Darien but he'll travel to Panama City for several days every month. He tells me that he is 22 years old and that he has studied at university for six years. Unlike his fellow tribesmen, he sports jeans and a blue plaid shirt, as well as a binder and address book. A blue chrome pen shines from his shirt pocket. He is the only one in the village wearing shoes — stylish white sneakers.

Oh well, I might not have attended the election meeting, but I did get an interview with a leading candidate.

*   *   *   *

With my map in hand, I wander to the meadow by the chief's shack where I first swooped down onto Púcuro. I want to plot my route for tomorrow's hike to Paya.

A bunch of men are kicking a soccer ball. They ask if I want to play. I decline and sit beside a boy at the end of the field to watch the players, though I sit warily because, when I was a schoolboy, every type of ball seemed to sail into my face no matter where I was.

The lad beside me is holding a flower.

"Where did you get that flower?" I ask him.

"My girlfriend gave it to me," he says, though he couldn't be more than nine years old.

"How many girlfriends have you?"

"Ten."

I wonder whether this isolated jungle hamlet even has ten girls around his age.

One of the soccer players dashes past me with the ball. "I found your knife on the trail," he cries. "You can have it back for five dollars."

Hmm, so this guy found my knife. Well I certainly can't afford to give him five dollars for it, especially for something I already own. Perhaps I'll trade him my sunglasses for it. I'll speak with him later.

I stare at the sky. Ominous black clouds are floating overhead, trapping the steamy heat within the jungle and oppressing its inhabitants.

Suddenly a thunderclap shatters the air.

Wow, I haven't heard one of those since I arrived in Latin America three months ago. My neck hairs shiver, not because it might rain, but because "the rains" might come — the endless, torturous downpour that turns the trails to mud-traps and floods the rivers for months.

The dark clouds sink lower. "I do have many girls," the boy beside me persists, "all over the world — including in China."

At the top of the field, the men scurry after the ball, then one kicks and it soars past the goalie and crashes into a banana tree. As the sun disappears completely, the goalie tosses the ball back onto the field. One player runs after it down the sideline, but both he and the ball end up chasing a duck, which flaps along in fright and finally dives beneath a shrub to escape.

He blasts the ball at the net, but the goalie grabs it in midair. "Good save," the men shout. Then they run back toward me to chase some chickens off the field, their thick bare soles pounding the ground.

The boy beside me is now fingering a dead lizard he has found. Once again the ball sails toward the net. "Enter! Enter!" they urge.

Now a cool wind preceding the deluge sweeps across the field. The heavens grumble. I stand and swiftly return home.

The children at the shack are hurriedly covering baskets and sacks with a tattered black tarp. In the shack across from us, several of the villagers are holding a prayer meeting. Outside the big hut in the village center, two women are hurriedly beating corn into flour.

The wind begins to rip through the village, bending the palm trees and flinging coconuts to the ground. As I stand underneath the shelter, stray mangoes roll across the dirt from one end of the village to the other. The gale intensifies, wrenching the mighty palm trees like twigs. The women still beat the corn, though the wind sweeps much of it away.

I wait and watch. I even muse that the deluge might have already burst from above and is at this very moment storming toward the ground — to slap the dust at any second.

The congregants in the prayer meeting shout praises. The windstorm whips up the dirt. Anything lighter than a mango lifts into the air and bounces off the shacks.

Another thunderclap splits the air. The children scream with excitement. The dogs bolt into the houses with tails between their legs. At the edge of the rainforest, massive branches tear from the trees and plummet to the ground. It's five o'clock and Mama dips a ladle into the cauldron to taste the dinner.

The wind stirs the fire into a rage. At the big hut, one woman persists beating the corn as her hair whips wildly. Now people are running from the fields into their houses. Dust and smoke from the fire choke my eyes.

The rains are on the verge of striking the earth. Swinging in the gusts, my hammock prepares to be attacked by the downpour. Children start to bawl. In the prayer meeting, the jubilation reaches a crescendo.

Banana leaves and sheet metal fly down the trails between the huts. The tarp covering the baskets flies away, taking a duck with it, then it plummets downward at the other end of the village and envelops an old man sitting in a chair.

Suddenly drops of water strike the dust. The torrent arrives!

As the first raindrops smack the ground, the chaotic wind ceases. No deluge appears. Instead a mere drizzle falls over the jungle for a few minutes as if to say "This is just a warning. You were unprepared so I neglected to unleash my wrath. Yet the rains, the real rains, shall soon arrive."

Evening settles over the village with a misty halo of soft light. The horizon fades to crimson, inflaming the wispy clouds. "Well, looks like there's no bus here to Colombia tonight," I joke to myself.

Slick swipes my sunglasses to try on. I tell him that the shades are not for the evening but for the bright of the day. Tomorrow I will try to barter the sunglasses to get my knife back. After all, the jungle is not bright, but eerie dim. I need the knife more than the shades.

When I return to Toronto I will buy another pair of sunglasses. From my suburban home I will take the bus and the subway downtown. I will observe the people — a different people than live here. I will buy my shades from the sidewalk vendors outside the Eaton Centre. Afterward I will enter the sprawling mall and watch the people walk by — those people of the "first world" instead of the "third world." When I enter a shop I will inadvertently speak Spanish when I ask for something. Every hour of every day for the past quarter of a year I have spoken only Spanish, and I will automatically speak it when I return to the first world and only after a while will I automatically speak English once more.

I stop ruminating on the first world and the subways and the affluent shopping centers and the ice cream cones. My mind returns to the jungle where majestic blue birds are rising from the cooling canopy and fluttering overhead toward the river.

The rain has long passed and the wind has long passed. Fruity scents fill my nostrils. The chatter of monkeys saturates the tranquil air. The candidate is sprawling in my hammock chatting with the electorate.

As I spit on the ground and wipe my nose in my shirt (my most convenient hanky) I wonder whether I'll ever become clean again. After this expedition will I even comprehend cleanliness?

Luis emerges from the prayer shack in a spotless white shirt. He joyously stretches out his arms and beams at the evening sky, feeling spiritually refreshed. Rick follows, wearing thongs and blue jogging shorts. They amble over and sit underneath the shelter, prattling in the Kuna tongue. After a while Rick turns to me. "Hey, I thought you were gonna leave this morning."

"No, tomorrow morning."

"Oh yeah. Hey, what are you doing — writing a letter?"

"No, I'm writing a book about Central America and I find myself scribbling a lot about this place."

"Oh, can I have a copy when it's finished?"

"Sure, just look for it on the bestseller list when you get back to the States," I quip.

The candidate listens to the conversation, then he looks at me and compliments my Spanish. After the missionary leaves, the candidate turns to me and murmurs, "This missionary with his big rich house hampers my purpose here."

* * * *

Looking like a colossal red pie plate, the sun sinks behind the treetops. The youngsters tell me that it goes to sleep in a cave. But not Slick — he remembers from his high school lessons where the sun goes at night.

Some of the children offer to trade molas with me. I barter a plastic watchstrap and lighter for one big mola, which I'll give to my mother back in Canada. To ease the weight of my pack for tomorrow's hike, I even trade away my mini alarm clock. The woman I give the clock to can't believe the generous deal she's getting.

The children start passing gas and giggling like the natives in Unión de Choco. The mother of the house asks me what I think about gas. I tell her that since I'm Canadian I know very little about passing wind. "Nonsense," she spouts. "All of the world passes wind."

The children tell me that the path to Paya and then to Colombia will bristle with tigers and savage boars. Then they offer to boil an egg for me for ten cents. Then they decide I should pay 15 cents. Their parents have trained them to squeeze me for every penny. Then they say that if I want tea with the egg the price will be 50 cents. I give them a dollar bill. They make the snack, but neglect to give me my change, hoping I'll forget about it. They've masterfully adopted the malice of their parents. They don't even consider mercy, kindness, justice. Instead, with every opportunity they swindle me for as much as possible.

Unfortunately we've developed a bitter relationship, these Kuna and I. They contrast with the shy, generous Choco. During the day this family jubilantly praises the Lord, but when night arrives they call you devil if you don't pray before eating, then they try to extort your money. Sadly their hypocrisy and greed present me with a poor impression of these people. At least I can sleep under this shelter for free.

Now the girl is demanding money from me for cooking what her mother told her to cook for me. My presence here is unmasking the worst of these bitter people. It's best that I'm leaving in the morning.

The girl now challenges me to prove I fear God. "Show me your Bible," she barks.

Then the woman I traded the clock to reappears. "The battery is ready to die, isn't it," she snaps. "That's why you traded me your clock."

"The battery is not ready to die," I reply calmly. "It will last many months."

"Liar. I don't believe you. The battery is ready to die. You're a liar."

The villagers soon retire to their beds. I climb into my hammock. In the morning I'll leave eagerly for Paya.

*   *   *   *

By breakfast time the extortion of my money climaxes. They sell me a meal of fried bananas for one dollar, a meal that probably cost them only three cents to make. I grudgingly render the charge, but this time I grumble that I don't overflow with money as they

138

might assume, but that I actually travel on an austere budget.

As I'm chewing my fried bananas, Luis summons one of his boys. He mentions something about ten dollars. The boy stares at the ground and begins fidgeting. Whap! Luis smacks him in the head. Then again and again he pounds his head and his back, pulverizing the child to the ground. After about a minute he relents and walks into the shack. But then he emerges with a leather strap and begins whipping the child like an ox, screaming at him as he writhes in pain.

The family sits nearby. But throughout the beating they look not at the wailing child; their eyes fix on me. Deep in their glare I perceive a hatred — their wrathful minds blaming their problems on the foreigner in their midst.

The beating ends and the mood lightens, and the family plays a game that everyone enjoys. They grab a dog and yank his tail until he yelps in pain, then they punish him for yelping by smacking him. The game grants smiles and laughter to all.

I resolve to retrieve my lost knife and leave this place immediately to resume my trek.

I fasten my pack and snatch my machete. The mother calls out to me. "You owe us another four dollars because we let you sleep here and we guarded your belongings from thieves."

Her demand astounds me. She suddenly wants to extract another four dollars from me for allowing me to sleep under the shelter and for watching my stuff from thieves even though Luis invited me to string my hammock here and even though I was the one that watched their stuff against thieves. I give her the money, not reluctantly, but eagerly because I've acquired a loathing for these deceitful extortionists and I want to flee this place. I don't even mention the 50 cents in change the woman knows she owes me from before; I leave the guilt for that on her conscience.

Even though I lost only a few dollars, I determine not to allow myself to be ripped off again. Their corruption reinforced to me another one of life's lessons. In the future I'll insist on determining the payment beforehand. Afterward is too late.

I hoist my pack and ask the boys to bring me to the house of the man who found my hunting knife. They lead me toward a hut at the other end of the village but they appear fearful of walking too close to it and they retreat. I strut up to the shack alone, clenching my machete, furious over the villagers' greed. My fury intensifies when I consider that this guy has my knife and it is mine and I want it back.

A man appears beside the hut. I ask whether he has my knife. He fetches it from beside a tree. I seize it from his hands and slip it into the sheath attached to my pack.

"Where is the five dollars for returning it to you?" he demands.

"You want me to pay you five dollars for something I already own?" I snap.

Before I can move he swipes the knife out of the sheath. "Fine," he says and he walks away.

I watch him march away. Though I am raging mad, I ponder whether to charge after him and forcibly take what is mine. But I think that fights are bad and we would certainly erupt into a fight and he has a hundred other villagers here who already abhor me because I'm not one of them. I pause, then walk off steaming, muttering about "that thief."

I wander over to the missionaries' shack to say farewell to Rick. He offers to lead me to the trail to Paya. I mention my dispute with the knife thief. He seems a bit embarrassed of the extortion by somebody who might be a member of "his flock." But maybe it will give him good sermon material.

We traipse to the opposite end of the village where the river gently curves. He points across the water to a patch of dirt among the banana trees. "Right over there — that's where the trail to Paya starts."

I shake his hand. Then I splash across the river and up the path into the banana grove.

The narrow trail winds peacefully under the morning shade of the bulbous banana trees. After walking for several minutes I notice a lone man chopping wood a few dozen feet off the side of the trail. My bitterness toward the knife swindler gives me an idea. I stop and withdraw my notebook. Because he swiped my knife I no longer need its sheath. I scribble "The thief has my knife, therefore the thief needs this too. Thank you thief — have a happy life in your profession." I fold the note and slip it inside the sheath. Then I walk over to the man beside the trail. As I approach he looks up.

"Good day," I say, then I hold out the sheath. "Can you please give this to the chief when you return to the village?"

"Certainly," says the man.

I reckon that the chief will know enough to give it to the swindler who has my knife. This man is old and small and looks kind. Maybe he has lived enough years to have learned that the bad and corrupt ways are wrong ways and that they bring unhappiness. He will probably return to the village for lunch in a few hours. But I decide to hike swiftly in case he returns earlier and the note angers the thief and the other villagers and they decide to pursue me.

I resume trekking. I ruminate that, when given the opportunity, even the oppressed will oppress. I'm losing faith in this world and its dastardly nature.

The trail widens and straightens. Within minutes my face dribbles with sweat. As I struggle up a hill I hear gunshots pierce the air behind me. I quicken my pace.

THE PROPHET

Eventually the impenetrable foliage on the right gives way to a sandy 100-foot bank embracing a wide river. Aside from the gurgling of the water far below, the daytime rainforest lies quiet.

The sun is rising toward late morning. The water I drank earlier is now oozing through my pores, soaking my back and running off my chin.

The trail widens slightly and climbs. After a few dozen feet the river on my right disappears and the dense foliage reappears and once again envelops me in a dark green tunnel.

I push on, refusing to pause for breaks. Once again the trail becomes tiring and monotonous.

Unfortunately you don't appreciate the magnificence of the jungle when you're deep inside it, swatting mosquitoes, gushing with sweat, desperate to fall on your face for half a minute to ease the exhaustion. I push on. To combat my boredom I blow drips of sweat off the tip of my nose. With practice I can eventually blow the drips three feet ahead of me.

The path suddenly veers right and descends. After a few hundred feet the path veers even more sharply and submerges beneath a glistening stream. I tumble down the bank and step into the water to cool my feet.

My compass hangs on a string around my neck and rests on my sweaty chest. I lift it to check the heading. Good. I'm on target.

I wade across the stream and resume hiking. Within half an hour I reach a picturesque bubbling blue river. I check the compass again. Hmm, the heading doesn't look good. Hopefully it will improve.

The directions indicate that I won't encounter any more rivers for a while. I lower my pack and reach into the water for a drink. So many tiny fish are darting around in this river that I inadvertently scoop some into my hands and almost swallow them. In fact, the word "Panama" is supposedly a native word that means "many fish."

I decide to bathe and shave. After stripping my clothes I step gingerly into the pebbly riverbed. As soon as my foot touches the water a slender transparent fish swims over to me, probably mistaking me for a fallen mango.

The warm current caresses my tired feet. The water rushes so swiftly that I have to restrain my comb and my soap under my toes.

I shave my ragged whiskers. Twice. Then I scrub thoroughly, enjoying my first bath since Unión de Choco at the beginning of the expedition a week ago.

I redress into my filthy clothes, then I sprawl on a boulder and hum a Springsteen tune. Many days of walking lie ahead. Colombia still seems distant. I'll photograph these clothes when I return to Canada, then I'll discard them. I gaze into the tranquil deep-blue sky and wonder when I'll be back in my homeland.

As I lie on the rock, midday arrives and the blistering sun peaks. I started hiking soon after dawn. The trek to Paya supposedly takes only six hours. That means I should reach the village in a few minutes. Why do I already envision myself still wandering through the bush deep into the afternoon?

I stand up to ford the river. Just as I put my foot in the water I see three natives beyond the opposite bank trekking toward me. They remove their boots and cautiously wade through the hardy current. When they reach my side they put on their boots and greet me. They tell me that they hail from another Kuna village and they're heading for Púcuro.

As they resume their journey I venture into the rushing waters. Midriver, in the swift current, I lose my footing and nearly spill over to float downstream. But after a few more feet of struggling I reach the opposite bank.

*   *   *   *

In my travels through Latin America over the past three months I usually relish a place when I first arrive, but within a few days it becomes familiar and I yearn for something new and I abruptly leave. Here in Darien, no matter how much I yearn for somewhere else, I can't abruptly leave.

I force myself onward. After every excruciating hill I resist the craving for rest, despite my ponderous backpack and waning strength.

I accelerate to a swifter pace through the wide tunnel that flutters with bees and butterflies and swarms with ants that carry delicate golden flower petals.

The jungle displays so many different personalities: the sparser hill-country around Pinogana; the awesome river canyons upriver from Boca de Cupe; the deathly dark mystical tunnels between the Choco land and Kuna land; the thick peat-smelling menagerie of deafening groans and squawks before Púcuro; and the gorgeous and treacherous rivers, those surging bloodstreams of Darien.

As I trek onward I see a crumpled piece of white paper on the path. I pick it up and unravel it. Scribbled in blue ink are four New Testament scripture references. Intriguing. I'll have to look them up later in my Bible.

I decide to rest here for lunch. I gratefully ease off my painful pack and sit in the dirt, so weary that even the enormous dead insect that's belly up beside me doesn't trouble me.

I examine my maps and wonder when I'll finally reach the coastal town of Turbo and the resumption of road. I figure I'm more than halfway through the expedition now. But I'm eager to reach the Katios Park ranger station to travel by riverboat once more.

Through the foliage to my right the river gurgles. I'll eat now and then really push onward. Man, I despise that massive backpack.

I try to open a can of beans but the opener keeps slipping and slashing my hand. Finally I bend apart a gap wide enough to dip a spoon into the mushy brown mess, and I reluctantly devour a few spoonfuls.

As I shuffle through my knapsack, a few fragments of granola spill out onto the ground. Almost instantly an ant scurries over, hoists a grain atop its head, then marches away.

I recline on the forest floor to rest, oblivious to the insects crawling over me. When I reach Paya I'll carefully measure how much food I'll need and I'll trade any surplus. I don't want to haul a heavy load over the killer hills of the Colombian frontier.

I resolve to resume hiking. But just as I'm ready to stand I look back on the path and see a man in the distance walking toward me. A hiker. It's another hiker. It's a balding gringo with a big backpack. As he approaches I notice that he's wearing a giant white t-shirt. No, it's not a t-shirt — it's a large banner draped around his neck. An expedition banner? No, not an expedition banner. The balding hiker is just a few feet away now and he's staring at me and pinned to his shirt is a banner that reads "Christ Is Coming."

I sit gaping at him. He halts in front of me and drops his pack to the ground. Then he smiles warmly and says hello. He sits beside me, exhausted from the jungle heat, probably figuring that now is as good a time as any to take a rest.

For a while we each sit quietly, saying nothing. Then I hand him my opened can. "Would you like some beans?"

"Oh, thank you. Yes, I'd love some beans."

He wolfs down the brown sludge. After a few mouthfuls he looks up and says, "Umm, son muy bien los frijoles." He pronounces very poorly and I discern that his Spanish is minimal, about the same level as the Swedes'.

As he feasts on the beans I notice another banner hanging on his back that also reads "Christ Is Coming."

"So what brings you to the jungle," I ask warily.

The man stops eating the beans, looks at the ground, and becomes somber. Then he faces me. "Well, since you have asked me what my commission is, and since it is my duty to proclaim my message, I will tell you."

He pauses to prepare his thoughts, then proceeds. "I am a prophet from God. I am walking around the world as a witness to spread the message the Lord revealed to me.

"God tells me where to go and he supplies my money. I set out from my home in San Francisco last year with 30 dollars. So far I have walked from California up to Canada, across Canada, down through the United States again, and down through Central America, walking all the way. I had no money for an airplane ticket to South America so now I am walking through this rainforest down to Colombia where I will continue my journey and my witnessing."

I sit dumbfounded as the man continues chattering. He says he had no worries about starting his world journey with only 30 dollars because he has faith, and so far God has provided for him. He says he travels on about one dollar a day, spending most of that one dollar on bread.

Then he elaborates more on his commission. "I am one of the two witnesses of the Apocalypse, described in the Book of Revelation. I can reveal this to you because I have been called by God."

He tells me that he and another witness will culminate their journey in Jerusalem. Once they arrive, the Beast of the Apocalypse will rise out of the abyss and slay them. But both he and the other witness will have power to turn water into blood.

I ask him what church he belongs to. He explains that he has belonged to many churches and holds many of their teachings. He bemoans that his mind mixed all their theologies together which confused the message God gave him, but he assures me he eventually sorted out a true theology and now has true understanding.

"I will recite a prophecy to you that God revealed to me in a dream." As we sit on the rainforest floor under the mossy canopy, his voice softens and quivers. His hands shake. He begins a lengthy oratory that makes me wince. "...and the trees are moving..." he proclaims "...and the rivers turn to blood..." And so his prophecy proceeds, detailing horrific apocalyptic destruction.

My neck hairs shiver. I have studied many philosophies. I have sojourned around the world; in the last three months alone I have explored many nations and even experienced several war zones. And now here I am deep in an isolated rainforest, in a no-man's-land between two continents, where a skinny, ragged man is reciting his sacred prophecy to me and claiming to be a holy man of God.

A NEW TRAVELING PARTNER

Since we're both hiking to South America, we decide to stand up and resume hiking together. We continue down the trail.

As we walk "the prophet" tells me that he when he reaches Jerusalem at the end of his journey he will be shot and lie in the street for three days before being resurrected. He tells me that he already journeyed to Jerusalem a few years ago and spent all his money there because he believed he was to be martyred. But he claims that he wasn't martyred during that excursion because it wasn't yet the proper time.

Now that he has found another person who speaks English and listens to him, he is chatting zealously. He tells me that God's Holy Spirit puts information into his heart. Now he is preaching that the ancient goddess Diana became Mary the mother of Christ. Then he goes on to explain that pop cans, shoes and televisions are part of the apocalyptic Beast described in the Bible because they don't biodegrade.

Then he begins preaching about the biblical symbol 666. "The number 666 refers to the Universal Product Code, or UPC found on retail items. When decoded, the UPC symbol equals 666. In the near future everyone will own a bank card with the evil 666 UPC symbol. They will need the bank card if they want to buy or trade."

Bermuda shorts cover the prophet's spindly legs. Underneath his banners he wears a white shirt that is embroidered with leaves and berries. His shirt has ripped in parts and been sewn together with red thread, which he says symbolizes the blood of Christ. He seems about 30 years old.

He tells me that he walks alone, seven days a week, from sunrise to sunset. "Sometimes I get lost on purpose as a test of faith because I know that God will guide me to safety."

As we wind along the trail, he continues rambling about his commission. I listen intently. While he walked through America, people often stopped their cars to give him money. Some even gave him 100-dollar bills.

Now he's talking about the other witness walking around the other half of the planet. "Who is this other witness?" I ask.

"I don't know. I've never met him. I just have faith that another witness like me is walking around the rest of the world and he'll meet me in Jerusalem."

Suddenly I remember the bewildering scrap of paper with the scribbled scripture references that I found on the trail a few minutes ago. It couldn't have come from this prophet because it was on the path ahead of him. I pull the paper from my pocket and show him. "Yes. God must be giving me some messages," he concludes. "I'll have to check those scriptures later."

The prophet and I push onward through the midday heat. Although the hours pass, his rambling perseveres. "To give me wisdom I mix myrrh into my toothpaste," he explains.

Occasionally I pose a question to him, usually about religion, to hear what he says. I notice that he sometimes seems at a loss for an answer and on the spur of the moment he decides what to respond.

As our conversations continue I'm stunned to discover that he actually passed through my hometown in the Toronto suburb of Mississauga along Lakeshore Boulevard, just a few miles from my parents' house, and that he can vividly and accurately describe neighborhoods familiar to me.

We pause for a break. Even though "the prophet" exudes the strangest banter, he does have a useful topographical map from the Geographic Institute in Panama City. I borrow it to make a slightly more accurate compass bearing.

Meanwhile he checks the mysterious scripture references in his Bible. The first scripture is in the Gospel of Matthew, chapter 28, verse 19: "Therefore go and make disciples of all nations, baptizing them in the name of the Father and of the Son and of the Holy Spirit..."

The second is in the Apostle Paul's first letter to the Corinthians, chapter 15, verses three and four: "For what I received I passed on to you as of first importance: that Christ died for our sins according to the Scriptures, that he was buried, that he was raised on the third day according to the Scriptures..."

The third is in the Acts of the Apostles, chapter 19, verse four: "Paul said, 'John's baptism was a baptism of repentance. He told the people to believe in the one coming after him, that is, in Jesus.'"

The last scripture is also in Acts, chapter two, verse 38: "Peter replied, 'Repent and be baptized, every one of you, in the name of Jesus Christ for the forgiveness of your sins. And you will receive the gift of the Holy Spirit.'"

"Hmm, these scriptures speak of baptism," he remarks.

We resume trekking. He continues babbling. As we walk I notice many good rocks here for sharpening knives. Before today I had found the good rocks only around water.

The afternoon lengthens and we struggle onward. I'm too weary to wonder about this bizarre new traveling partner.

The trail swiftly dips and we stop. In front of us is the third river crossing of the day. We stand dripping in the thick humidity.

The river has carved a corridor through the treetop canopy. Far above us loom black rainclouds. Thunder claps the air. The heavens begin to drizzle.

"Let's cross the river and get moving," I urge, envisioning a deluge and possible flooding ahead. We arduously wade through a stronger current than I've felt in any of the previous rivers. Then we enter the semi-dry tunnel on the other side and hike forward.

As he talks further about his life, I begin to understand more about this man I've found myself traveling with. "I don't really want to talk about high school," he confides, "but I'll tell you about it."

He discloses that his school made him visit many psychiatrists who gave him drugs that caused objectionable side-effects. As he recounts his story, I grow sad because I learn of the tragic and confusing adolescence he suffered. I grow to understand that this self-proclaimed prophet appears to be a mentally-troubled man, emotionally scarred, deluding himself with self-glorious fabrications.

"Sorry for talking so much," he says. "I'm hyperactive because I've met someone who speaks English. Let me know if my talking starts to annoy you and I'll stop. By the way, my name is Mark."

"You can call me Andrés," I reply. " — or Andrew in English."

*   *   *   *

The drizzle spits through holes in the canopy, but we remain fairly dry. Despite the rain, the jungle air remains hot. I wonder whether these are the summer rains — whether the wet season has actually begun. But today is only April 5th; the torrents shouldn't burst forth until later in the month.

Mark tells me he worked in San Francisco as a bicycle courier and as a chef. As we plod along the narrow root-mangled path he details his favorite dessert recipes. "...then you freeze the bananas, blend them with milk, sugar and thick cream and then freeze it again." Then he describes some more of his favorite foods. "Try freezing chocolate milk, it tastes great." Next he recites pie recipes. "...wrap the pie crust around ripe apples or pears and bake one hour."

He's beginning to madden me with all these images of delectable desserts, especially since my only nourishment for the near future will be rice and boiled bananas.

As we push over the hills, Mark continues to preach — not about prophesy now, but about the joys of homemade pizza and lemonade. Even as the sun sinks toward the horizon he continues to jabber, now about pie recipes again.

Since he's babbling so intently and since he stares at the ground as he walks instead of looking around him, he doesn't even realize that the dense bush has faded and given way to banana trees. I happily announce that we've almost reached Paya. Still gazing at the ground, oblivious to our new surroundings, he eagerly returns, "Yes, we'll probably be there soon."

The trail widens. Then we hear a river gurgling a few feet beside us to the left of the trail. As we continue, the river grows closer until we see it beside us, shallow and rocky. As we traipse alongside the shore, the river suddenly curves right and blocks our passage. The trail halts at the top of the riverbank. A bridge, hewn from a monstrous tree trunk, spans the river in front of us. At the other end of the giant log, a smooth hill of red earth rises from the frothy water and splits the one river into two. A few dozen crooked huts stand atop the red mound, glowing orange under the setting sun.

We have arrived in Paya, the capital of the ancient Kuna kingdom.

Our tired eyes smile at the delightful village at the other end of the mighty log.

"Alright!" I exclaim. "We made it to Paya!" whereupon I begin to cross the log.

"Just a moment," says Mark, fumbling around in his metal-frame backpack. "I have to be wearing my banners before I enter a village."

The last sliver of tangerine sun slips below the canopy as Mark pins his "Christ Is Coming" signs onto his shirt. We stride over the wide and well-worn log to the rolling red hill on the other side.

One of the village men greets us and directs us to the chief's home, describing it as a large hut at the fringe of the village by the water's edge. As we walk through the ancient settlement, the residents smile and greet us. Good. The Kuna here seem friendly. They'll relieve the sore impression I developed from the grouchy Kuna in Púcuro.

We follow a small path beside the river and find a large hut surrounded by trees and bushes. A man wanders out and introduces himself as the chief. He invites us into the hut and tells us we can sleep here tonight. In gratitude I give him a few cans of frijoles.

The hut is the village meeting place. It's a long, narrow shack about the size of a bus. Inside, a bench lines each wall. Aside from a small log-hewn table with a couple of chairs just inside the entrance, the interior is empty.

The chief invites us to share the evening meal with him, and he walks off to tell his cook to prepare two more portions.

Mark and I drop our packs to the floor and lie on one of the benches. I stare up at the leafy ceiling. Drizzle begins to fall once more, punctuated by flashes of lightning and booms of thunder. I peer at my watch but the inside of the glass face has fogged over and I can't read the time.

A young boy loiters around the shack and watches us. Then he disappears and returns a few minutes later with a pair of glowing specks in his hands. Fireflies? I walk over and look. No, a pair of magical black beetles with luminous green orbs.

"Where do you find them?" I ask

"At night — down by the river."

Mark and I gaze at the glowing insects. Then the boy abruptly squeezes them dead and watches for the next minute as their luminescence expires.

The chief returns and tells us that someone is bringing the meal shortly. Then the boy suddenly points to the dinner table and cries out. "May I borrow your machete, please," the chief asks. I hand it to him. He marches over to the table, pushes aside my notebook with the blade, and slashes a black lump beside the oil lamp. "Spider," he says. "Very venomous."

With the spider dead, we can sit down to relax and chat before dinner. I ask the chief whether he has traveled beyond the Darien. He tells me that he has visited Panama City and that he also journeyed to

Medellín in Colombia where he studied science. "I too plan to visit Medellín," I disclose. "How is it? Is it big?"

"Yes, Medellín is beautiful, with many tall buildings." His report excites me. Since leaving Mexico City, the biggest city in the world, three months ago, I've mainly traveled through mountain villages and small towns and the small Central American capitals. Now I'm swooping down onto a new continent — a mega-continent with giant countries, immense populations, and vast metropolises like Bogotá, Caracas and Sao Paulo.

The chief turns to Mark, probably wondering about his banners. "Tell me, what is your profession?"

"Well, I used to be a bicycle courier but now I'm a prophet."

"Oh," says the chief skeptically.

I erect my hammock. Like the Kuna in Púcuro, the man examines it with awe and delicately climbs into it. His son jumps in after him and lies between his legs with his feet up his father's nose.

Mark is so appreciative of the chief's gracious food and lodging that he presents him with a postcard and a bar of soap. Then he retreats to his backpack, retrieves his air mattress, and inflates it. I stay reclined on the bench, watching the astonished expression of the boy as he observes the expanding air cushion.

The woman preparing the meal comes into the big hut holding the can of frijoles I gave them. She asks me whether they're sweet and whether she needs to heat them before eating.

This talk of food spurs Mark into more recipes. So hungry am I, and so deprived of rich North American cuisine, that I begin frantically scribbling down everything he says.

"One day get a bunch of assorted vegetables and cook them in olive oil over a low heat." He also describes a taco recipe using beans, mashed potatoes and jack cheese. Then he urges, "Try chicken and peaches covered with plum and banana sauce." All that this man talks about all day is food and prophecies. And here I am madly scribbling his recipes! "For banana pancakes," he continues, "combine whole wheat flour, bananas, cinnamon, water, eggs, margarine and raisins. But it's the bananas that really make it. If you want you can freeze the pancakes and eat them later. Of course you can use cherries instead of bananas."

Finally the woman emerges with steaming plates of rice, boiled plantain and a half-dozen delectable fish that taste like chicken except for the hard, black crust. We eagerly devour the meal. After we finish the food she brings each of us a mug of supersweet tea — it's actually just sugarcane juice with a tea bag plopped inside.

Our dinner now finished, the chief wishes us good night. I settle into my hammock and Mark settles into his air mattress.

I've learned that we're actually sleeping in a meeting hall of the ancient yet still-thriving Kuna Congress. There are numerous local Kuna congresses, and also a General Congress for all the Kuna people. With its democratic tradition, the Kuna Congress has been described as the grandmother of parliaments. The chief moderates the assembly. He is an elected leader.

In the 1920s the Kuna people fought for and won semi-autonomy from Panama. The Kuna manage most civil and criminal cases themselves and only involve the Panamanian government for the more serious legal matters.

The European explorers who met the Kuna half a millennium ago were surprised by the egalitarian government — a system founded on radical principles like freedom of opinion, making every vote count, and equality for all humans. Kuna women also retain much authority in Kuna life. For instance, when a Kuna man marries he goes to live with his wife's family. Kuna women also own and inherit land.

Some say the explorers' revolutionary accounts of the Kuna government helped spark democracy in Europe.

Today only a few hundred Kuna abide in Darien's interior, while another 40,000 populate the San Blas islands off the eastern coast.

As I gaze at the leafy roof of the meeting hut, my fatigued body relaxes and I drift asleep. My last thoughts ruminate over the excruciating dawn-to-dusk hike to Cristales in the morning. Today's hike ravaged me; tomorrow's hike will stretch much longer and prove far more brutal.

*   *   *   *

When I wake at dawn, my mind is still visualizing the crushing trek ahead of us today. But I slept well and I feel rejuvenated and keen to start hiking.

Since embarking on my excursion through Darien I've developed a habit of falling asleep when darkness descends and waking at sunrise. Even though it's only 6:00 a.m. I feel eager to rise. Moreover when you lie all night in something like my lightweight hammock, which is only barely comfortable, you sleep only as much as you need. You don't want to stay in it more than you have to, so you avoid oversleeping. It's an effective anti-laziness contraption.

Mark has already risen. He is squatting on his mattress to squeeze the air out, while sewing his ripped shirt with his red thread. He's not talkative now. Perhaps he has exhausted his reserve of recipes and prophecies.

Today is Thursday. If I can reach the Cristales Ranger Station tonight then I might be able to catch a riverboat to Turbo tomorrow morning. But that's a best-case scenario, something I haven't yet experienced on this expedition. It's wiser to envision and plan for the worser-case scenario.

The worser-case scenario entails two full days of hiking to reach Cristales (assuming we don't get lost — it's not only the longest and most brutal part of the trek, it's also the trickiest to navigate).

Hopefully we'll slip across the Colombian border before sunset tonight. I'm purposely neglecting to imagine what might befall us once we pass into Colombia. Will we fall into the treacherous hands of jungle bandits? Or guerrillas?

Prophet Mark has developed a bizarre plan of salvation to use if evil men confront us. First we keep our money well hidden. If bandits accost us, we tell them that seven of our friends are just a few minutes behind us. Then we just be polite and humor them. After 25 minutes we yell "Jesus Christ!" which will frighten away all the bad men.

"Andrew," says Mark, "would you mind if I traveled with you all the way to Turbo? You know how to travel around here and you don't get lost. I'd really appreciate it if I could tag along with you."

"Sure," I reply. I would actually prefer to travel solo but this prophet seems helpless and he doesn't know how to navigate. I'd feel guilty leaving him to fend for himself.

I roam around the village to take some photos. After getting about ten good shots, one of the native men approaches me and asks me about my travels. He's especially interested in my experiences in Nicaragua. By the time I stroll back to the hut, most of the village is buzzing about el periodista — the journalist in their midst.

I bid good morning to a girl standing near my hut. When I ask her how old she is she says, "Nine." When I ask her how many siblings she has, she stares into the sky for a few seconds, then finally looks back at me and replies, "Plenty."

Mark and I gather our belongings and prepare to resume our hike. For the first time since Panama City I strap on my hidden money belt beneath my shirt and stash my cash. If the stories of the banditos and guerrillas and killer cats of this region prove true then this might be the most dangerous day so far in my three-month journey through Latin America.

* * * *

According to the hiking directions and the chief, before we begin the trek to the Colombian frontier we have to journey about a mile upstream to a shack alongside the river where some soldiers are stationed to interdict "mules" — outlaws ferrying cocaine from South American labs into Central America. We must show these Panamanian soldiers our passports before trekking the last few miles to the Colombian border.

I decide that I don't want to spend a whole 20 minutes hiking to the Guardia post and another 20 minutes hiking back here before our trek for the day even begins. After all, they'll only write my name in an immigration book. So I ask Mark to go ahead and take my passport with him, telling the soldiers that I didn't come because I have sore feet.

Mark complains that he's feeling a bit weak so I give him a can of frijoles. Then he sets off while I stray in the village. I want to try to get some kind of breakfast or at least get somebody to cook some oatmeal for me.

When I return to the hut, the kids are eating fried bananas dipped in the frijoles I gave the chief last night. The woman tells me to sit at the table. Soon she presents me a breakfast of rice, eggs and sugarcane tea. After eating, I give them a colorful lighter as a gift for providing me breakfast.

Mark returns. Instead of hiking to the Guardia garrison he went searching for more food. His arms overflow with bananas — not hard, green plantain but real yellow bananas. We sit down and eat them, then I give the family here some of my cheese. We've developed a good relationship, these people and I. They freely give to me and I freely give to them. There's no haggling or arguments, and the children here sit in my lap and play with me instead of telling me that I'll go to hell because I haven't said grace before taking my soup.

Mark finishes his bananas, jumps up, and sprints off to the soldiers' station. Meanwhile the chief recounts more about his village. He tells me that an evangelical missionary once came here from Canada and stayed for 11 years. He also boasts that his language is the easiest language in the world to learn.

I examine Mark's topographical map, which provides much more detail of the terrain than the hand-drawn map that I have from my guidebook. But the more I scrutinize the map the less I trust it. The map doesn't even show Unión de Choco or the settlement we'll encounter at the Colombian border. But the contour lines and river markings prove helpful. They confirm that today's trek will be rugged all the way. The first half of the hike will be uphill and the second half downhill. The map stops at the Colombian border, but I figure it will take at least two grueling days to reach Cristales inside Colombia, and we'll encounter very few rivers where we can obtain drinking water.

From the map I can determine that the elevation here in Paya is roughly 100 feet above sea level. To the east a mountain range named Lemon Heights crests at about 1500 feet.

To build up my strength I brush the bugs off another banana and devour it. Soon Mark returns from the army post, but with bad news. The soldiers say both of us must come to the post in person, and we must come with all our gear. They're holding our passports until we return. Mark is shaking from hunger. I feel weary and I want to rest a bit in my hammock but the chief is sprawling in it again. "Okay, there's nothing else we can do," I decide. "Let's take our bags and go so we can get this over with and start our hike."

Carrying our backpacks, we start walking toward the Guardia post along a narrow trail following the river, slightly to the east of the trail that brought us into the village yesterday. The river is called the Paya, like the village it surges past. Originating in the no-man's-land in the verdant eastern mountains, this shallow and rushing water eventually merges with the Tuira River and ultimately empties into the Pacific Ocean.

After about 20 minutes, Mark points upstream across the river to a cleared area with a shack. "I'm not bringing my camera stuff and my money over there," I declare. "If they inspect our bags they might swipe some of my valuables before sending us on our way."

I stash my daypack with my camera and cash behind a bush across the river from the shack. Then we ford the frothy waters.

Dressed in shorts and t-shirts and brandishing M-16s, the soldiers direct us to sit at a log table beside the river. The senior officer examines my passport. After finding the exit stamp I got from the proprietor of the supply store in Boca de Cupe, he writes my name, nationality and passport number in a book and returns the passport to me. "Your documents are in order," he mutters. "You're free to go."

I wait as he examines Mark's passport. Then the problems begin. "Where is your exit stamp?" the officer demands. "Exit stamp?" replies Mark, who turns to me in confusion.

"Didn't you get your passport stamped at the supply store in Boca de Cupe," I ask.

"No, I didn't know I had to do that."

"Oh boy, this is going to be a problem." I pause to think. "Well, don't worry, somehow we'll resolve this."

The officer is still scrutinizing us, waiting for an answer. "He passed through Boca de Cupe," I explain, "but he didn't know he had to visit the supply store for an exit stamp."

The soldiers look at one another, unsure what to do. This is likely the first time they've encountered this problem. On the one hand they can't disobey orders and allow him to pass into Colombia without an exit stamp — after all, he might be a fugitive. On the other hand they don't want to send him on a six-day journey to Boca and back just to get a stamp. And even if they did order him back to Boca, he could easily disregard their order and simply hike past Paya into the no-man's-land and into Colombia.

For almost an hour we sit around, with everyone trying to imagine a solution to the predicament. Finally I envision a possible resolution. "I have an idea," I announce to the soldiers. "According to your will, permit this man to leave. When he enters Colombia he can visit the Panamanian consulate, explain what happened, and set his documents in order, thereby resolving the problem."

The officer considers the proposal for a few seconds, then pronounces it reasonable. "Very well," he says to Mark. "We will let you leave. But as soon as you get to Colombia, visit our consulate there and explain what you did."

"Okay," says Mark eagerly, thankful that he has been freed.

The officer scribbles some information about him in his book and then hands him the passport. We thank the soldiers and wade back across the river. Once we're back on the trail, I snatch my sack from its hiding place behind the bush.

We march back to Paya.

*   *   *   *

After crossing the log bridge back into the village we ask a boy to show us the path to Palo de las Letras. He leads us down the side of the red hill and downriver a few yards, then he steps into the water. "Follow me across," he urges.

We step tentatively into the current. About 50 feet wide, the river ripples over slippery rocks. Halfway across, with one foot sliding on a mossy rock and the other foot sinking in mud, I realize that the treacherous rapids have engulfed me. What a fool I am! Before stepping into the river I should have wrapped my camera and money in the waterproof bags I have, but I was too lazy. Now the river threatens to fling me over and carry me downstream. I don't give a hoot about myself — I'm fretting over my 1000-dollar camera and my 900 dollars and my three months of scribbled notes.

Mark has waded a few feet upcurrent. His face clenches in fear as huge whitecaps slap his back and he strains not to slip under. We begin hollering at each other over the roar of the waters. "Come on up here! It's easier," he bellows.

"No!" I yell back. "Don't cross there — you'll slip away."

Mark lifts his pack atop his head and labors through the silver plumes, one wary step at a time. The Kuna boy is treading in front of me, with huge gushes of water lobbing over his shoulders. As I slowly push toward the opposite bank, an enormous four-foot long banana leaf surges downriver toward me, wraps around my leg and tries to pull me downstream.

Finally we reach the bank and stumble through a few feet of mud onto a dry path.

"One dollar please," says the boy.

"What!" says Mark. "You didn't tell us you wanted a dollar to take us across the river." Mark's daily budget on his worldwide journey is only a dollar a day, so he's fuming. "You didn't tell us anything about us giving you a dollar," he continues to scold. "I'll give you the money, but you must tell people beforehand that you are going to charge them money to bring them across. We didn't need you to bring us across. We only needed you to point to the path. We can cross the river ourselves."

Mark fishes out a soggy dollar from his bag and hands it to the child, who walks off belittled from the scolding but pleased with receiving his fee. Feeling sorry for poor Mark I reach into my money belt and offer him one of my dollars. No, he says at first, but after a while he grudgingly takes it.

I sit down and examine the wounds I've received in the past few weeks. My foot pounds from a thorn that stabbed me last night. Cuts cover my arms because I sometimes balance the machete on my neck as I walk, to keep my hands free, and it occasionally falls and nicks me. I also scorched my forearm a few weeks ago at the border between Nicaragua and Costa Rica, but the wound is healing. I received the burn just after I cleared Nicaraguan customs. During political tension between the two countries, their immigration posts were built a mile and a half apart at the main border crossing on the Pan-American Highway. After passing the last Nicaraguan checkpoint, I began walking down the road toward the Costa Rican checkpoint. But after I had walked just a few hundred feet, an 18-wheeler truck finished its customs inspection and began slowly rumbling down the road toward me. Reckoning this might be an opportunity for a free ride down to the border post, I stuck out my thumb for a hitch. The truck didn't slow for me, but the driver yelled out the window. "Come on up! Jump on!" I ran alongside the cab, grabbed a handle and lifted myself up. As the truck sped up and my hair began blowing happily in the breeze I suddenly felt my arm on fire. I pulled it away from the cab and swung to the side — my forearm had been resting against the scalding muffler. In the next few days the skin bubbled, but the pain soon left and now the wound has almost healed. Though the burn from the truck is from a few weeks ago, it now seems so distant — like it's from a past life — my pre-Darien life.

I examine Mark's map once more and take a compass reading. At least we won't confront any more rivers to fall into. But that means we also won't confront any more rivers to drink from. We take a long last guzzle from the Paya and fill our canteens. Then we don our packs, take a final glance at the pretty, friendly Kuna capital, and begin walking. Soon the sounds of the village and the sounds of the river fade and we're tramping through a sweltering, winding jungle tunnel.

Midday passes. The twisty path has climbed steadily since we began hiking in the early morning. Perhaps we'll reach the border by late afternoon.

Sweat has thoroughly soaked my clothes. Another thorn has slashed my foot through one of the numerous holes in my ragged shoes. New water blisters have appeared on my foot, just like the ones that disabled me in Unión de Choco. My pack straps have become impregnated with grime and my salty sweat. I drank the last of my water long ago, my throat has become parched, and neither the map nor the terrain indicate any rivers for many more hours — perhaps not even until tomorrow. Nevertheless an adventure is an adventure and an adventure is definitely what I'm experiencing.

We pause to rest. Mark babbles about the Book of Revelation. Somewhere in the foliage an armada of bees drones. We eat some cheese and save some for bartering.

"I really want to keep traveling with you," says the prophet. "You can bargain for riverboat passage for us and you'll bring us safely to Turbo." This man is so timid. What a person to be traipsing halfway around the world on a religious mission.

We discuss more tactics for evading danger once we pass into Colombian territory. At my request Mark agrees to stop jabbering when we reach Colombia so we don't attract whatever might be lurking for us. "Actually my only worry is that the banditos or guerrillas will rob me and torture me," claims Mark. "It is impossible for me to die until I am martyred in Jerusalem."

After we rise from our rest, I feel that I have only enough energy to continue hiking for about one hour, yet we have at least five hours of trail ahead of us. Hiking in Darien is different than hiking in a cooler high-latitude forest. Here I'm blistered, suffering from heat exhaustion and occasional sunburn and dehydration, while carrying a cumbersome overloaded backpack.

I'm just living day by day — my only goal is to swig another ounce of water, to devour another morsel of food, to reach another sunset, to sleep deeply when night falls.

The journey has become so endless that at times I can't even envision escaping the sweltering rainforest and reaching Turbo. My imagination's furthest reach is tonight; for now that is my only goal — to reach tonight. And by this evening I will triumphantly celebrate that I hiked all the way to Colombia.

We continue plodding. Giant roots repeatedly trip us; at least once every five minutes I snag my foot and nearly smack my face into the ground.

The path develops into a painfully slow rollercoaster, dipping and rising. The bottom of each dip always reveals a creekbed — always a deathly dry creekbed.

*   *   *   *

Mid-afternoon. My condition deteriorates. Though I'm trembling with weakness I push on.

The sweat. I can't even describe the abundance of sweat. How can a person perspire so much and survive? Then, when you stop to rest, the slight breeze from walking fades, so the sweat flows even more. My sole desire is to push forward and find a river. Yet I don't expect a river, no matter how much I yearn. The terrain here won't support one. We have crested into highlands, far from any water.

My feet ache. I walk quickly — fast or slow it's still the same number of steps so I prefer to walk quickly and arrive sooner.

A cut behind my ear (where I carry my machete) is stinging from sweat. My middle finger also has a rusty red line of blood.

We pause to clean the grit from our shoes and socks and toes. Four o'clock arrives. No sign of Palo de las Letras. Ignoring pain we push on, pushing our bodies to the limits though they're screaming to stop. Although my condition is deteriorating, it is a slow and steady deterioration that I can monitor.

Since my Darien expedition began, I have almost ceased urinating — maybe only twice a day, just a few dark orange spurts, a sure sign of dehydration. I start to fantasize about the big city of Medellín in Colombia — all the soda and lemonade and beer I will drink to compensate for the half month of thirst in the bush.

*　　*　　*　　*

Halfway to the border, supposedly several hours ago, we should have hit a river. But we saw nothing, unless we were too overcome by our dehydrated stupor to notice.

Mark's map doesn't show every river — only the larger ones. It doesn't show the cool, rushing shallow rivers with delicious water, inhabited only by fish, and far from any banana field or village.

The trail dips once more and we meet another dried creek. Wait — the soil feels moist, not sandy. Look! Over there the loamy creek bed is supporting a stagnant black puddle from last night's drizzle. Tongues hanging out, we dip our canteens into the murky mixture, then I drip a drop of bleach into each cap and we shake. Then we drink. It tastes marvelous, no matter how nauseating it tastes.

I peer at the treetops. What a magical world this is! A bee stings me, but it adds little pain to my already throbbing aches, which I've now grown accustomed to.

We rest. The prophet pulls out his New Testament. He says the Lord tells him to study it thoroughly because one day he will be writing part of it. Every few minutes he looks up and offers me words of wisdom. "The Lord prefers compassion to sacrifice," he informs me, followed a few minutes later by, "Love is the most important."

Mark tells me that when he was in Mexico some cops robbed all his money. He adds that he has been cast out of many towns because he often preaches on street corners. But he also says many people treated him kindly in Central America. Often when he was walking along a vast stretch of highway, with the same bus drivers passing him every day on their routes, they stopped and offered him free transport to the next city.

He also says that whenever he reaches a border checkpoint the officials are already expecting him because days beforehand motorists tell them he is coming.

The heat begins to fade. In a few hours the evening will encroach. I feel better after drinking the puddle water. We stand up and march on.

The trail continues to twist through endless highlands, the same gentle dipping and rising, the same chattering green tunnel.

My throat becomes parched again. Sweat drenches my clothes. My cuts ooze blood. My body still begs to stop. But we persevere.

As the evening robs most of the already dim light under the canopy, I wonder whether we'll even reach the border before nightfall. Then as we round a curve I glance ahead and see a curious boulder blocking the trail. We approach cautiously, then stop in front of the rock, bewildered.

I drop my pack and walk around it. "Look!" I whisper to Mark. He walks over to me. We stare at a thick, aged metal plaque resting on the side of the stone, engraved with one large ornate word — "COLOMBIA."

My watch reads 6:17 p.m. Today is the sixth of April of the year 1989. We have reached Colombia. I hand Mark my camera and he snaps a photo of me standing beside the stone, tattered and tired, my backpack at my feet.

Night begins to fall. We don our packs, energized by the victory of reaching the frontier. But now we must continue. Tired and hungry, we must find the settlement that's supposed to be here at the border.

"Remember, Mark, no talking. We've entered Colombian territory now. Remember the stories of the banditos and the guerrillas. They might be just a few hundred feet away from us right now." Mark nods his head.

With me in the lead we sprint along the trail through the cool evening, wondering where this settlement is. The path leads downhill. My heart pounds as I envision bands of marauders lurking around each bend.

Suddenly I stop. Mark crashes into me. I listen. "Voices. I think I hear voices," I whisper to Mark over the throbbing of my chest. "Maybe not — I don't know. Let's keep moving."

We dash farther down the trail. But in the encroaching darkness we keep tripping. I stop again, panting. "Mark, I don't think there's a settlement here. We're in the middle of nowhere and there's no river for miles. I don't know. I thought there was supposed to be a village or something here but there's no sign of anything — no bananas, no smoke, no water.... I don't think any village exists anywhere near here."

We decide to dig in for the night. I traipse off the side of the trail and slash a small clearing with my machete to make camp.

Darkness surrounds us now. I fix a candle in a crevice between two branches — I figure any guerillas in the area will likewise be settling in for the night by now and won't wander by and see the light. At least that is what I hope.

I string my hammock between two trees. Mark erects his pup tent, crawls inside, and inflates his mattress.

As the jungle chatter increases, I sprawl out on the hammock. Through cracks in the canopy I see strings of stars twinkling in endless loneliness, separated from me by a million light years and by a thick, mossy ceiling a few feet over my head.

The nearest village lies seven torturous hours behind us. The closest road is much farther behind us, six days to the north. Here we have only ourselves, our backpacks and a bone-pervading solitude.

The candle burns steadily. Rodents and snakes rustle through the leaves beneath me. As the moon climbs higher into the blackness, a pack of monkeys howls from the treetops. Then I hear a sound I've been dreading.

Back in Púcuro the natives told me this was the most dangerous territory of the rainforest. They say that the pumas roam fearlessly in this area because even their hunters don't venture this far. They said if I make it through here then I will make it through Darien.

I hear the sound again — a heavy tromping. What is it? As I squint through the darkness I catch a glimpse of a black shape slinking behind some bushes. In the jungle night you hear everything and see nothing. As I peer through the foliage I glimpse a burly black beast. Or do I? I'm not sure what I see. Yet what my eyes can't see my ears can hear — steady, heavy footsteps are advancing toward me!

I strain to hear. The husky footsteps pause — then continue, circling the perimeter of the camp just beyond the candlelight. I shine the flashlight, but it's useless — the light glances off a wall of leaves and back into my face.

My machete is resting beside my right hand, inches from my grasp. If a jungle cat attacks me I have decided on a strategy. Just hold the blade in front — if he attacks he will leap into it and impale himself. The machete is all that I need. It's also all that I have.

The footsteps circle behind me. Then I hear heavy breathing a few feet behind my head beyond some bushes. My heart pounds, pounds, pounds. I gently crane my neck to see, trying to move as quietly as possible. Silence for two minutes. Then the footsteps slowly retrace to where I first heard them. Another pause. Then the steps retreat into the squawking jungle darkness.

My thumping heart relaxes. But I don't sleep. As the night advances, pandemonium erupts. Mosquitoes and fireflies surround me. Bats whiz a few inches over my face.

The clamor increases — screams, yowls and ravenous growls in the distance; ripe and heavy fruits falling from the branches and slapping into the moist earth; most hair-raising of all, the occasional sound of large animals crashing through the bushes around me.

Wow! What a fantastic place. But slumber doesn't come easily here. Not until three in the morning do I finally drift asleep.

* * * *

I wake with the first slivers of the orange sunrise. My candle burned faithfully through the night. The mosquitoes departed about an hour before dawn. I wish I had brought an insect net to cover me. My face

179

and head bristle with bug bites, although my weariness and heatstroke and dehydration have ceased.

I climb out of the hammock. Anticipating the blistering heat just a few hours from now, I strip off my pants. They'll only hinder me. I'll just wear my shirt and underwear. Besides, I've grown so slim these past few weeks that my trousers no longer fit — I have to hold them up with one hand as I walk so they don't fall off.

Mark emerges from his tent. He divulges that during the night God revealed to him two morsels of knowledge: the Lord told him to read The Hobbit, by Tolkien, and the Lord told him to read War and Peace, by Tolstoy, because they supplement understanding of His Scriptures.

Mark wants to begin trekking. He says he always walks from dawn to dusk. We open a can of tuna and eat hastily. My only remaining food is a can of sardines and a bag of granola.

We tear down our simple camp. Since we're starting so early we have the advantage of walking through the cool of the day. Hopefully we'll find a river soon. Aside from yesterday afternoon's puddle water, my last drink was a night and a day ago when we left Paya. On the cheerier side of the news, I wander behind a tree and joyously expel my first bowel movement in days, probably encouraged by yesterday's stagnant water.

I estimate that we'll reach the Cristales ranger station by noon. Maybe we'll find a riverboat going downstream soon after we arrive. But there's certainly no village around here — just endless green jungle with a thin brown ribbon to walk along.

I raise my canteen to my lips and swallow the last of my puddle water before we set off. Then I look around me. Hey, this is stupendous. I actually made it to Colombia! Wow, to think I might see road again within a few days.

The morning light gradually penetrates the flora. We slip into our packs and stand. This will be my last day of hiking — I know it — it has to be. Soon there will be riverboats and villages and we'll travel down the estuaries and through the Great Atrato swamp and down into the mighty Atrato River.

I take hold of my cool machete handle, moist with morning dew. I start moving forward, wincing, my legs brutally sore, my back aching. But I'll push on, because tonight the hiking ends forever — just a few more hours to freedom.

* * * *

After less than an hour of walking I falter and collapse. The endless trudging and the dehydration and the lack of sleep last night have traumatized my body. I'm suffering from a permanent yawn that wants to shut me into eternal sleep. Yet I retrieve my notebook from my pack and delicately scratch, "I'm pushing on — I'm going to make it."

I stand and we hike forward. I don't even want to stop for rests anymore — I'm afraid I won't get up again.

One foot in front of the other. One foot in front of the other. And Mark talks and talks and talks.

"Stop!" Mark yells out. He looks at our arms. "We're infected by ticks!"

I blink at him, bewildered. I've never suffered a tick infestation before, so this is new to me. But Mark knows what to do. "Take off all your clothes," he orders. Then with both of us standing naked in the middle of the trail he starts plucking little black dots off my back and buttocks and instructs me to do likewise to him. What a sight we are! Two men standing naked in the depths of an isolated rainforest, plucking bugs off each other's bare butts.

Soon we've removed them all. "We'd better keep walking," he urges. "We'll probably get re-infected because they're probably in our clothes and our backpacks. We won't be able to get rid of all of them until we reach civilization."

We resume hiking. Within a few minutes I can feel them tingling in my underwear again. "There's not much we can do," Mark continues as we walk along. "We can't get rid of these ticks. They'll lay eggs inside you and you'll have an outbreak."

As we wind around giant tree trunks I meditate on my life. Most parts of my body ache. Lumps, bites and cuts cover me. I haven't slept well in ages. And last night a puma (or some other big beast) stalked me in the dark.

Mark is right. Within a few more minutes my socks itch with the ticks. They emerge from nowhere — suddenly appearing on an arm or between fingers.

A few minutes later the prophet abruptly halts and hands me the dollar bill I gave him yesterday morning after we crossed the Paya River. "The Lord told me to give this back to you." I decline, but he insists, and I reluctantly take it. This journey is too bizarre.

THE PATH ENDS —
IN THE DEEPEST BOWELS OF DARIEN

We continue to stagger along the slender trail. We haven't heard any voices or seen any trace of human inhabitance, yet we continue to whisper — just in case. Then, as we stumble down a rooty hill, a fabulous sound tickles our ears. "Listen, Mark — I hear a river!"

As we eagerly bumble down the path, the trees clear and a silver stream appears. We drop our packs. I wade into the current and lower my face into the water and drink, and drink, and drink, and drink.... After filling my belly, I strip my shirt and splash my face and chest. Then I wade back to my pack, my gut sloshing with water.

We fill our canteens. Then we sprawl by the bank and rest for a few minutes, allowing the water to rejuvenate our dehydrated souls. After a few minutes we rise and ford the stream to continue along the trail. But when we reach the opposite bank we stand baffled. "Hey, where does the trail continue?" I exclaim.

We walk up and down the bank looking for the path. But we find nothing but dense jungle. To make the scouting easier we splash up and down in the creekbed. Finally we find a path a few dozen feet downstream. Why it resumes there I have no idea. I don't even know who or what made these wild and twisty paths through this immeasurable menagerie.

We continue hiking, refreshed by our drink. The trail winds around giant tree trunks that rise from pungent soil the color of moist coffee grounds. Within a few minutes the path descends and another river appears.

We take another drink then stand in the river gazing around for the resumption of the path. But both of us suddenly freeze when we glance upstream and see a large man standing in the middle of the river about a hundred feet away clasping a long machete and staring straight into our eyes.

"Friends!" Mark yells at him in Spanish. "We're friends with you." I tighten my grip on my machete. But within a few seconds I see that our meeting has stunned the big man as much as it has stunned us. Slowly and cautiously we approach each other.

"Hello," I say. "We are travelers. We are journeying to Colombia — to Cristales, then down to Turbo."

"Ah yes," replies the man, adorned with black trousers, a blue t-shirt, big rubber boots and a tiny bag slung over his shoulder. "I am traveling to Panama."

We stare at each other for a few moments. "How much longer to Cristales?" I ask.

"About three or four hours. I left there at sunrise today. You will find riverboats from there to Turbo for about three dollars."

Then he asks, "Will I meet any Guardia on my way into Panama?"

"Yes," I respond, "by Paya, the next village you'll encounter. But not along the path — off on a different path."

"Okay," says the man hastily. "Good journey."

We watch as he splashes over to the trail and disappears into the foliage. We find the path and continue trekking. I should have asked the man whether any guerillas roam the area and how long the riverboat journeys to Turbo will take.

*   *   *   *

Mid-morning arrives and we ford two more rivers — the third and fourth of the day. But after trudging through the fourth river we lose the trail again. I sit to rest and to write in my notebook. Mark scouts up and down the river to find the elusive path.

After Mark has been gone for about ten minutes I look across the river and think I see a trail behind some bushes. I wade over and look, but find nothing but a tiny rabbit track that dwindles within a few feet. I hear Mark sloshing behind me in the river. "Nothing up that way," he reports.

Together we scour up and down the riverbank, peering into the flourishing green collage, finding nothing. Almost an hour of searching passes; then I hear Mark hollering downstream. "Down here, Andrew. I found the trail down here."

I eagerly squeeze through some bushes to climb down into the river again, but I slip and slide down the rocky bank and shred my left forearm. As I sit defeated with my butt in the warm water I decide that I've become nothing more than a walking injury.

I splash downstream to Mark and we climb the bank and move forward, aching to reach Cristales.

*   *   *   *

Soon we stop to rest once more. Mark no longer takes out his New Testament to read the Book of Revelation. He simply sits on the path and plucks his ticks.

The jungle has become cool and quiet and it fills my nostrils with the fragrance of ripe fruit — all hints that the sky might drizzle once more. The numerous rivers we've already encountered today in these lowlands contrast with the dry highlands of yesterday. We stand up and continue southward, my shoes glossy wet and my belly sloshing with water with every step. I still haven't adjusted to being in Colombia. I have to keep reminding myself that I finally made it.

The terrain becomes more arduous — gouged by deep ravines and steep climbs. After slithering down 20 feet into one ravine I moan, "Let's stop and eat the sardines, Mark."

We sit beside the water and open the tin revealing the tiny bed of smelly fish soaked in tomato sauce. "I generally don't like sardines," claims Mark, "but maybe they'll taste good in this sauce."

We each chew down a few, then I pass the rest of the tin to Mark to finish off. "I don't like them very much," I grimace.

"Me neither," winces Mark. "But I'll eat them for the energy."

After finishing the fish, Mark turns to me soberly. "You know I'm really grateful that we can travel together. No matter where I travel, God always provides me some kind of a guide to lead me through difficult places to safety."

We climb the opposite bank and continue down the tiny path. My body aches so much now that I wince from simple maneuvers like ducking branches and lifting my legs over roots. During the lengthy climbs I scream inwardly for a few minutes to push myself to the crest, then we stumble down the other side for the next few minutes — endlessly up and down and twisting around. But mid-afternoon is approaching and I feel we will soon encounter the ranger station.

The afternoon endures along the never-ending path. As we plod along, I suddenly notice something smooth and black at the side of the path. "Look, Mark. What's that?" I walk closer. "Wow, I don't believe it. It's a tire!"

We stare dumbfounded at the battered ring of black rubber. "Why is there a tire here? Why is there a tire here?" I keep repeating. "We're in the middle of nowhere." Finally I offer the only possible conclusion. "Nobody would roll a tire in here — it must have dropped from a plane." (Later I deduce that it was probably a remnant from the failed Corvair expedition of the early 1960s.)

We leave the tire behind and once again resume trekking. Mark wants to get to South America as soon as possible so he can continue his witnessing to the world.

Eight hours have passed since we saw the man who said Cristales was four hours away. But no Cristales — just endless green bush and unending clamor above and around us.

The fiery afternoon fades and evening approaches. Then at about six o'clock the trail widens and we meet a broad rushing river.

I look at the map and the hiking directions. "This is it, Mark — this is the last river. Just a few more minutes to go!"

We ford the river. "Wait," I urge, "I want to brush my teeth. I haven't brushed in ages." Mark pauses as I fetch my toothbrush and paste. I methodically clean my teeth, then once again I fill my belly with water.

We push forward. This is it. We're almost there. We've almost made it. Then no more hiking — we'll soon travel by luxurious riverboats, hewn from jungle logs and filled with sacks of bananas.

The trail winds madly through sparser forest, brutally up and down. Hyperventilating, I nearly faint. "Mark, I have to sit. I'm gonna faint. I can't go on. I need to rest for a couple of minutes."

We pause and my panting relaxes. I feel like waiting behind and letting Mark continue onward. I lie on the path. Then a roar rips the air. "An engine!" I whisper to Mark. "That's an engine. Cristales must be just past those trees down there."

We stand and start running, but I feel like collapsing. "Mark, run ahead. It must be the big river and a boat. Run ahead and see if the boat is going to Turbo."

Mark dashes forward for a few seconds, then timidly changes his mind, probably considering the horror stories of the guerrillas. "I'd prefer if you run in front," he stammers.

With me leading, we rush forward, careening around bushes and ducking branches. Suddenly we emerge in the warm evening sun in a small grassy clearing. A few feet in front of us, two husky Afro-

Colombian men are standing beside a diesel-powered electrical generator with wrenches in their hands. Behind them is a white shack. Beside the shack, alongside the river, stands a large wooden sign: "Katios National Park."

"Hello," wave the two men, who promptly return to their tinkering. We walk over to them.

"Is this the ranger station?"

"Yes, it is," says one of the men, his head inside the engine.

"We want to go to Turbo. Will there be a boat traveling there sometime soon?"

"Maybe. But not tonight. But you can stay here until a boat comes."

"Can we buy some meals from you?"

"Yes, talk to the man inside."

We amble over to the cabin and climb onto the front porch. Another man comes out and greets us.

"Can we stay here and buy some meals from you until a boat arrives for Turbo?"

"Yes, you can stay. You can sleep on the porch for free. Meals are two dollars each."

The meals seem expensive, but I don't care. We made it and I want a nice dinner to celebrate. "Are there guerillas in these parts?" I ask the man.

"No. There are no guerrillas around here."

We sit on the front porch while the man tells somebody inside to make dinner for us.

As we relax from our endless hike, three soldiers with backpacks emerge from the trail. I hold my breath momentarily, wondering who these soldiers are and why they're here. Then I see that they're Panamanian

Guardia, one man and two women. They greet the men by the generator, then they come over to the cabin and drop their packs. The man on the porch walks over to chat with them.

They smile at us. I find out that they came here from a different border area a few hours away, closer to the Pacific Coast. Mark starts chatting to them, explaining that he's a prophet on a mission from God. I wander away, leaving him to his preaching.

After a few minutes, the soldiers exchange some packages with the rangers. Then they put on their packs and stride back into the bush.

We trade some American dollars for Colombian pesos with one of the rangers. Then a plump woman with an apron appears and tells us to come in for supper.

We sit at a solid table and the woman brings each of us a plate of rice and chicken, with a glass of grape juice. I gaze around as I eat. This definitely isn't a shack; it's a sturdy cabin.

After the meal we pay the woman two dollars each and wander back onto the front porch. The sky ripens orange, then blossoms with streaks of scarlet. We arrange a riverboat ride with the rangers for tomorrow morning. But as we're negotiating with them we hear a droning downriver and a few seconds later a wooden canoe with two short native men inside pulls up along the river bank and ties up in front of the cabin.

The rangers greet the men and help them unload some supplies from the belly of the dugout. When they've unloaded, Mark and I stroll over. "Are you going to Turbo?" I ask.

"No, to Bijao," replies one.

"How far downstream is that?"

"About two hours."

"And from there we can find another riverboat going to Turbo?"

"Eventually."

"When do you return there?"

"We go now."

"Can you take us with you to Bijao for five dollars each?"

"We leave in five minutes."

"Okay, we're ready. Just let us bring over our bags."

We retrieve our packs and lower them into the middle of the dugout. Then we climb in and they fire up the outboard. Mark and I wave goodbye to the rangers and we swivel around in the current and gently motor downstream. Wow, this is great. Just an hour after reaching Cristales we find passage downriver.

*   *   *   *

The sternsman revs the motor, raising the bow a few inches and slicing a frothy path through the silky green water. The river is called the Cacarica. About 30 feet wide, she winds lazily through the half-light of dusk under a luminous light blue sky that glimmers with the first evening stars, but still burns orange along the western horizon.

My Darien odyssey began just eight days ago when the Swedes and I climbed out of the yellow pickup truck in the isolated outpost of Yaviza, deep in the lavish rainforest of southern Panama. Countless days and miles later, the hiking has finally ended. In fact we've actually left Darien proper. For the next few days we'll travel by riverboats through Colombia's Katios National Park, then through a rare sunken forest, then the Cacarica widens and penetrates the Great Atrato Swamp. Finally we join the voluminous Great Atrato River, a marine highway that wanders gently down to the Gulf of Urabá in the Caribbean Sea. Two hours across that gulf lies the port town of Turbo.

Tonight we'll lodge in this village of Bijao, which I know nothing about. In the morning we'll try to find passage to Turbo. If all goes well we might even reach Turbo by tomorrow evening.

DOWN THE CACARICA

The last remnants of evening light dwindle. I sprawl on my back on the bottom of the buzzing riverboat, resting my head on my pack. My heart skips with excitement and awe. I feel the boat lean as we weave around curves. Trees and dense bushes cover the banks and stretch over the water, forming an eerie tunnel that glitters with glowing green beetles.

Though we're speeding underneath a roof of sturdy moss-covered branches that droop with intricate vines, the trees yawn open in a few sections and reveal mesmerizing heavens twinkling with myriad stars. As always, howls and chatters emanate from beyond the curtain of leaves. And Mark and I don't even know exactly where we're going — except that we're heading south, the direction to eventual civilization.

As we propel downstream, the poler perches in the bow, blaring signals. "Log left...shallow right...." Every few minutes we shut off the motor and he poles us through a shallows. Then we rev the outboard again and rumble downriver through the darkness.

After about two hours of negotiating the river, I notice a clearing ahead on the west bank that supports a cluster of tilted shacks illuminated by orange torchlight. We motor up onto a muddy beach and clamber out to pull the canoe from the current.

After lifting out our packs I fetch a ten-dollar bill from my money belt and hand it to one of the men.

"Where's the rest?" he demands.

"What do you mean?" I answer.

"The passage costs 20 dollars each."

"What! Before we got into the boat I said we would pay you five dollars each to bring us to Bijao."

"No. The passage costs 20 dollars each."

Mark stands nervously beside me. "We'll just give them the money, Andrew. They're thieves, but we don't want any trouble here."

"No, Mark. We said five dollars each. I won't give them 20 dollars."

"Look, Andrew, I'll pay them the money — we don't want any trouble."

The scruffy men stare at Mark and me bickering with each other in English. "Don't pay them 20, Mark — it's a rip-off."

"No, it will solve the problem," Mark says as he fishes two 20s out of his wallet. "Look, I'll even pay for you. You don't even have to pay me back."

Mark hands the men the 40 dollars. They take their oars and climb the bank into the torch-lit village. "What a waste of money," I mutter to myself. "What a rip-off. That amount of money would have lasted me half a week."

We ascend the muddy bank into the village, which is nothing more than a couple of dozen shacks reeking of urine, crying with babies and flickering with oil lamps in the sticky night air. Barefoot and bare-chested men shuffle between the huts, barely visible in the night.

We stumble around the darkness in confusion. Eventually we ask one boy where we can buy some bread. He points to a larger shack at one end of the village. As we walk over to the shack we hear the occasional howl of "Hey gringo, what are you doing here?"

By the time we reach the shack, a clump of the locals is trailing us. We glance over our shoulders, growing more and more uneasy. After walking over a wobbly board that spans a urine-trickling ditch, we step into the dimly-lit store. Behind a plain wooden counter a middle-aged man's face flickers from the lone oil lamp, his dark body backdropped by a few shelves of canned fish. Several young men and women are slouching against the walls. The room silences and every gaze fixes on us. "Do you have any bread?" I ask politely.

"Yes, we have bread," says the proprietor.

"How much?"

He mutters a price in pesos, which I don't understand very well since I've never used this currency before. But I perform some quick calculations in my head and the price seems reasonable, even though I reckon he's swindling us.

We buy two loaves, then turn to exit the store. A crowd has gathered, blocking the entrance. "Excuse me," I say, and we squeeze past them to get outside.

"Listen, I don't like these people," I whisper to Mark. "And those boaters we argued with saw how much money we have. I think we should find somewhere isolated to sleep. Otherwise we might get mugged in the night."

Mark agrees. We wander back down toward the river to try to find a place where they won't discover us. We walk quickly and the crowd just looks after us, but doesn't follow us. We find a trail by the river where nobody can see us and we follow it a few feet downstream. "Look, there's a field," I say. We approach the clearing and look around. "Nobody can see us here. Let's just sleep in the field. Anyone trying to mug us won't find us there."

We climb over a barbed wire and follow a narrow path through tall grasses. After a few hundred yards we leave the path and traipse a few dozen feet into the pasture and set down our bags. "This is as good a place as any," I remark.

"Yeah, and safe too," adds Mark.

We smooth out some grass and lie on the flat ground under the cloudless midnight sky. Mosquitoes whir around us, occasionally nibbling our faces. "These mosquitoes are driving me crazy," mutters Mark after a few minutes. "I'm going to set up my tent."

"Can I come in with you?"

"Well, there's not really enough room."

The prophet struggles to erect his tent, but eventually gives up. "I can't get this thing up, and this bloody zipper is busted on the front door."

Mark decides to evade the insects by crawling inside the flat tent, but within a few minutes he gives up that as well because his face is suffocating under the nylon and the bugs still attack him in there as much as they were out here.

The bugs don't bother me as much. Besides, the shimmering night sky enthralls me too much.

After a few minutes I turn my head to the right to gaze across the field and I freeze in awe. At the other end of the clearing, just below the towering canopy, thousands of fireflies hover in the air, frolicking in the darkness. Above the canopy, many miles to the south, brilliant flashes of white light splatter the deep blue sky. Dumbstruck, I stare at the astonishing spectacle. Since there are no clouds tonight I must be witnessing a titanic electrical storm.

For the next few hours I watch the swirling fireflies and the distant flashes, drifting in and out of sleep, lazily swatting bugs in the tranquil midnight air.

*   *   *   *

Eventually the lightbursts dwindle and I grow accustomed to the dancing fireflies. As we enter early morning, the insects drive Mark into greater and greater frustration. At about 2:00 a.m. he begins singing old show tunes, claiming that they calm him. By 4:00 a.m. his voice is quivering with stress. He announces that he can't handle the mosquitoes anymore. "Andrew," he says softly, "I can't take it anymore — I can't take these mosquitoes." He pauses, then announces a radical decision. "I'm going to inflate my air mattress and drift downriver on it. At least that way I'll be making some headway. If you want you can come with me."

I persuade him that instead of floating downriver we ought to look for somewhere else to sleep with fewer mosquitoes. He assents. We gather our belongings and wander back to the soundless village and choose a spot beside some canoes where we find fewer mosquitoes. As I sprawl out on the ground beside a log, the first glimmers of dawn appear.

We close our eyes but can't sleep. Soon the village wakes. Babies begin crying. Mothers stoke the cooking fires. Villagers meander to the riverbank to bathe.

Mark and I stand up. He returns to the store to buy more bread. I decide to search for passage to Turbo. My impression of these people grows worse and worse when I discover that there's no shortage of people willing to bring us to Turbo, but the crooks are demanding anywhere from 80 to 100 dollars for the ten-dollar journey, knowing well that we're stuck here if we don't eventually give in to one of the offers. Each time one mentions such a ridiculous fee I just turn around without answering and walk off in disgust.

Mark reappears with the loaves. I tell him about the fares people are offering me. "It might be a while before we leave this place," I add. "Hopefully we won't have to give in to them. But if we don't find a good fare soon I think we should find a trail that leads downstream to another village."

The lack of sleep and the unfriendly surroundings drive Mark into deeper anxiety. He timidly sits and chews his bread. I wander through the village to find someone who will take us downstream for a decent price. I also want to sell my machete, because someone told me that the Colombian police will demand a juicy bribe from any gringo they see with one.

I approach a man by the riverside. "Do you know anyone traveling to Turbo today?"

He points to a dugout beached at the lower end of the village. "Ask at the boat over there that they're loading with sacks."

I saunter down the riverside trail to the slender canoe. "Is this boat going to Turbo?" I ask one of the men loading sacks.

"Yes, as far as I know."

"Is there space for my friend and me?"

"Don't ask me; I'm not going." He points to a short, middle-aged Afro-Colombian man in a red shirt. "Ask the Captain."

I trudge over to the captain of the boat, but by this point I've grown clever enough not to ask how much passage is to Turbo. Instead I tell him what I'll pay before he offers an edgewise word. "I understand that you are going to Turbo," I begin. "My friend and I are traveling there and we're wondering whether you can take us. Look, we will give you ten dollars each. That's 20 dollars for you." I reach into my money belt and pull out the bill and hold it out to him. "Here is the 20 dollars. What time do we leave?" Without saying a word he takes the bill from me and pockets it.

"We leave at eight o'clock sharp," he snaps, and walks off.

I dash back to Mark and narrate our good fortune of getting passage to Turbo. "Only ten dollars each," I extol. "I already paid him and we leave in half an hour. Wow, this great price makes up for getting ripped off last night."

On the offchance he decides to leave without us, we stuff our bags and bring them over to the boat and Mark waits among his sacks. I wander through the village and find a woman who says she'll buy my machete, but she offers a ridiculously low price. We both shake our heads, unable to settle on a compromise price. But a few minutes before the boat leaves, I barter just a few cents up from what she offered and we strike a deal. I only sell it for a couple of dollars, but I wanted to relieve myself of it before departing. I no longer need it.

Soon el capitán returns to his floating log and we push offshore and climb in. He yanks the outboard to life and we purr downstream. In addition to the owner and Mark and me, two women passengers are on board. All of us in the heavily-laden boat perch atop sacks of rice.

As we motor downstream, the women and the man chat with each other. Interestingly they append their sentences with the formal señor or señora. They also address each other with the formal nominative tense usted instead of the more common tú. And they also precede each other's names with the formal Don and Doña (for instance the women call the captain Don Miguel). Compared to the other Latin American countries I've traveled through, these people speak the most formal Spanish I've heard.

* * * *

One of the rainiest regions of the planet digests us into its marshy abdomen. The Cacarica develops into the most captivating river of the entire expedition. In this stretch she's nothing more than a slender vein of murky water meandering through a mystical sunken forest — a dense bog permanently soaking under a warm waist-deep soup. As far as I can view in every direction, I see nothing but wide trees sprouting from a glassy wet floor. In fact I don't feel like we're traveling along a river at all: I feel more like we're traveling atop a watery pathway through a ghostly ancient forest.

Every few curves the channel becomes too shallow and everyone clambers out and we push and pull the dugout through. We struggle through more shallow sections. Then the captain, for some reason, tells me to go up front to pull the rope while everyone else shoves from the sides and behind. Maybe he senses that I'm more industrious than the others — or maybe he just wants me to be the one to disturb any crocodiles or fall into any holes. But I don't mind. I feel good with the warm water caressing my legs and waist. I don't mind the twigs and moss and other unseen jungle lumps that surge past under the water and slap our legs. As we nudge the boat over one difficult spot, I joke with snake-fearful Mark. "Boy, Mark, do you feel all those snakes floating past us and hitting our legs?" He returns a petrified expression.

At times the heavy log boat becomes so grounded in the shallow river that pulling won't pull us through — we have to bend over and dig a path. I stuff my cheap digital watch into the breast pocket of my ragged shirt, but a few minutes later when we bend over to dig out of a rough spot the watch slips out of my pocket and plops into the muddy current. I don't even bother to feel around for it.

*　　*　　*　　*

About two hours after our departure the river widens and deepens. We motor smoothly downstream.

Soon the forest thins. I see bright light downstream. Then we burst from our sewer-like tunnel into a sunny marsh. The captain relaxes the motor and steers us to starboard into the reeds by the southern bank. We slow to a stop beside several men sitting in a half-dozen bigger canoes.

Mark and I sit patiently as the men greet each other and chat for a while. "Very dry," I hear the captain reporting to the others. "She is very dry and very difficult." I determine that the swamp is like a transfer point for goods. The small dugouts negotiate the shallow, narrow passageways through the sunken forest, then they meet the larger canoes here in the deeper water and swap cargo.

The morning has drifted past ten o'clock and the sun rages. After a few minutes the captain instructs us to take our bags and move into a bigger boat beside us. After tossing our belongings into the long red and white canoe, we climb aboard and wait. Eventually he climbs in behind us with his small personal sack and yanks the starting cord on the big outboard. The motor roars to life. He waves farewell to the other men and we begin moving downriver again, this time through deeper and wider green waters, banked by rustling swamp grasses and occasional thinly-leafed trees. We've left the rainforest behind and entered the Great Atrato, a swamp the size of Rhode Island.

* * * *

El capitán guns the engine, spewing silver sheets behind us. The smooth green band widens even more.

As the sound of the rushing boat travels ahead of us, regal white birds lift into the air and flap into the treetops.

The river continues to widen. Now she seems more like an endlessly long lake, or like the mighty Amazon, except that she's flanked by forests of reeds and thin sunken trees instead of a solid shore.

The unchanging scenery endures. I lie back and cover my face from the midday sun and fall asleep despite the perpetual engine drone.

When I wake an hour or so later Mark looks dejected. "I lost one of my shoes in the river," he moans. "I was just dipping into the water to clean it but it slipped from my hand."

"Didn't the captain turn around the boat to get it?"

"No, it was too late. It sank right away. The captain and I both waved goodbye to it as it went under."

I'm now traveling with a single-sneaker prophet. I can just imagine him hobbling up the road when we reach Turbo.

I sprawl out to sleep once more. When I wake again we're docked alongside a large river town. When I turn my head to the left I am stunned at the width that the river has grown to — maybe half a mile wide now. "We stop here for 15 minutes," the captain barks.

*   *   *   *

I climb onto the dock and wander around. I think this is the settlement called Puente America, meaning Bridge America. Back in the days when they still planned to complete the Pan-American Highway between North America and South America, engineers came here to stake out a mega bridge over the river and swamp that would finally link the two continents. But of course the highway plan expired and the bridge never came and the formerly-enthusiastic town lost its dreams of the span of asphalt that would ferry money-laden travelers.

As I roam through the town looking for a shop, I notice that the river runs along both sides of the village and I decide that this is an island. As I tread down one of the two dirt roadways lined with shabby shacks, I notice a Malaria Control Station and I sneak by quickly in case anyone sees me and nabs me for a malaria test. (Unlike most third-world tropical travelers, I don't take anti-malarial pills because I heard of terrible side-effects).

Soon I find a small store where I buy some biscuits and a cold soft drink. When I return to the boat the captain asks me to buy him a soda as well because he has to remain with his boat. He gives me an empty glass jar and I amble back and fill it with cream soda. When I return to the boat he thanks me but doesn't offer me any money.

We push off the dock and start motoring downriver again. I turn to one of the ladies traveling with us. Wrapped in a cool light-blue dress, she's about 35, with deep black skin. "What time will we arrive in Turbo today?" I ask her.

She laughs back at me. "Ha, ha — not today. Tomorrow morning."

The riverbanks now lie about half a mile away on each side. As we motor into mid-afternoon the shores drift even farther. After checking my map I notice that we've left the Cacarica and swooped down onto the voluminous Great Atrato River.

Also referred to as Cocaine Highway, the Atrato originates 400 miles to the west in the highlands near the Pacific. The lower 250 miles is navigable by small boat. She flows northeastward through the great swamp and eventually spills into the Gulf of Urabá on Colombia's Atlantic coast.

After so much time in the bush I can barely grasp the Atrato's breadth. I survey the distant shores as we speed northeast toward her ocean mouth.

The endless cruising down the endless smooth river endures into the soothing late afternoon. The sun relaxes. As we serenely skim the gleaming blue water, an affectionate tropical breeze massages our faces and tosses our hair.

The Atrato gradually narrows. Just before dusk a cluster of shacks appears on the northern shore, hovering on stilts over the muddy riverbank and connected by raised walkways of faded planks. The engine slows to idle and we veer toward a dock and tie up. "Just five minutes here," proclaims the captain. "Then we continue downstream."

Mark and I climb onto the dock and use a battered, bottomless outhouse hovering a few feet over the water. After using the outhouse, I tell Mark I'm going to see if I can find anyone to sell me some bread.

I plod up the plankways and approach a woman beside her shack. "Is there a place here where I can buy some bread?"

"Yes, I can sell you some bread."

She disappears for a few minutes then returns with two loaves. I hand her some peso bills, but she doesn't take them. "Oh my, I don't know whether I'll have enough change for those," she frets. "Wait here and I'll go and try to find change."

As she wanders away I hear Mark hollering a few houses away down at the dock. "Andrew! Andrew! Come back here quickly — the captain says he's going to leave right now."

"Hang on a second. I'm buying some bread and she's just looking for some change."

I stand on the plankway fidgeting for another minute then I hear Mark yelling frantically. "Andrew! Quick! He's leaving without you!!" When I turn to answer him I see the boat pulling away from the dock with Mark standing in the back waving madly.

I stare in shock. He wouldn't dare. He wouldn't dare leave without me. Just then the woman returns with a handful of change. He has almost turned the boat around into the current. I think of my bags — my every belonging sitting in the stern atop those rice sacks. "No, I have to go," I bark at the woman, whereupon I drop the bread onto the plankway and frantically run back to the dock, soon realizing that the planks act like diving boards if you bounce on them too much and the faster I run the more they threaten to throw me up into the air and down into the muck.

When I reach the dock the captain slowly motors back toward me. I clamber back into the boat and glare at him fiercely. "What did you do that for?! I was coming back over."

Fuming, I squat beside my bags. I wonder how somebody who just met me could be so malicious toward me at every opportunity. We reverse into the current and rumble downriver.

*   *   *   *

Rainforest once again shrouds the shoreline. Now that we've left the swamp behind, the river narrows to a width of about 150 feet.

The sky dims into a faintly glowing light blue punctured by the first pinholes of starlight. I stretch over the sacks and drift in and out of sleep in the muggy night air.

When I wake an hour later the outboard is grumbling slower. A black sky stretches from horizon to horizon and we're drifting toward a small string of lights along our port side. We swivel around and dock starboard.

"Everybody out," says the captain. "And bring your bags. We sleep here tonight."

We haul our bags onto the dock. We're at the mouth of the Atrato. A few hundred feet downstream the river drains into the Gulf of Urabá. Tomorrow a two-hour cruise across the gulf will dock us in Turbo. We leave at dawn.

As we follow the captain across a wide boardwalk I notice that he limps. He leads us into a warmly-lit shed, bare except for a desk and an old outboard on a stand and some engine parts piled in one corner. A hallway at one end of the shed leads into a family's shack.

We all set our bags down on the floor. A few minutes later a woman emerges from the hallway with a tray of tiny steaming coffee cups. She offers cups to the captain and the two women and then surprisingly turns to Mark and me and offers likewise. (I say surprisingly because, aside from the reasonable forest rangers, most of the people we've encountered since entering Colombia have treated us coldly, especially this crafty captain whom I mistrust.)

"I'm going to try to buy some bread, Mark," I say as I saunter outside the shed, still craving the poor loaves I dropped on the plankway in the other village.

I stroll up the battered but wide walkway. The outpost, whose name I don't know, is just a row of shacks and sheds about 150 yards long, nestled between the silky river and the dark, sultry rainforest.

In the center of the settlement I find a large and brightly-lit house that sells food. A friendly old Latina woman appears from behind the counter and greets me. The shelves behind her exhibit the abundant stocks of drab sardines and packets of sugar cookies that I also noticed in Puente America.

I buy a bottle of Coke and a packet of cookies and a bag of chips that says in English "with more real crunch." The civilization I'm accustomed to is not far away now.

Mark hobbles into the shop and buys a soda and, in his meager Spanish, recounts his gospel to the attentive proprietress. I recline into a plush chair by the entrance — aside from one chair at the Katios Ranger Station, this is the first comfortable chair I've sat in for weeks.

After guzzling my soda, I buy a couple of loaves and stumble back to the shed along the dark boardwalk, several times stupidly stepping through breaks in the planks.

When I reach the shed I don't go in because I'm not tired enough to retire for the night. Instead I start chatting with a middle-aged man outside the shack next door who is sitting in the evening breeze with his girlfriend. The husky-voiced chap is only the second white Colombian I've seen since entering the country. I ask him about Turbo, then I ask him what the dollar is trading for. I think for a moment. Because he has already given me a frank answer about the rate I ask him whether he'll exchange some dollars for pesos with me. He agrees and I trade a 20 with him.

When I return to the shack with my loaves, one of the women passengers asks, "Where did you buy that bread?" which are the first words she has spoken to me since we began our mutual journey early this morning.

Toward ten o'clock the captain and other passengers begin clearing away some of the dirt on the floor for their sleeping spot. Mark withdraws his air mattress from his pack and starts inflating. The others glare enviously. "Do you have one of those too?" one of the women asks me.

"Of course not," I candidly reply. "That is a luxury and I am a poor man."

We all sprawl on the wooden floor. Over the past three months I've adapted to sleep on anything — buses, boats, hammocks, fields. So the floor should feel comfortable.

My face and arms feel slightly sunburned; I guess my skin became too accustomed to the dim jungle — in fact I feel like I just spent a lifetime deep in the timeless rainforest. When I was in the jungle "civilization" seemed like a distant memory from a former life. Now that I'm returning to "civilization" the jungle already seems distant, part of my past, a mere memory. I'm still a wanderer, wandering from one land to another. I stretch out on the hard floor, using my backpack as a pillow, but grasping it with one hand in case anyone tries to snatch it in the night.

I drift asleep, trusting nobody, my switchblade secretly ready, once again surrounded by another unfamiliar outpost on this earth.

I wake at dawn with Mark's frantic whispering. "Andrew, get up — everyone has left." When I look around the room only one of the women remains. She swiftly stuffs her last belongings into her bag and shuffles out to join the others at the dock.

I stand up, lift my pack onto my shoulders, and trudge bleary-eyed to the boat. The captain sees me. "Get into that boat over there," he directs. "He will take you to Turbo."

"How much will he charge?"

He tells me the trip will cost only 500 pesos, about $1.25. I eye the other boat warily, wondering why the captain is discarding us. But seeing the other passengers climbing in I reckon that he's legit and I climb in after them.

Mark appears from the shed with his pack, but he hurries not toward us but to the outhouse. A young black man climbs into our big canoe and yanks to life one of the two sturdy black outboards on the stern. As he unties the docking ropes, Mark reappears from the outhouse and hobbles over in his single sneaker. "Ahh, excuse me, sir, how much is it to Turbo?"

"Just get in, Mark — we're leaving. It's only 500 pesos. Come on, get in."

After Mark struggles into the boat we push off. Just past the last shack the river expires and we spill out into the choppy gulf under a cool misty dawn. As we leave behind the jungle I stare ahead to the east, across the gulf, and see a sliver of land on the horizon. To the north and south I see nothing but turbulent gray water speckled with prodigious white seabirds and crowned with ominous black rain clouds.

Our new boat seems similar to our last one. Pale red and big enough to hold about eight people, she features two giant black outboards.

The pilot guns the twin engines, surging us over the ocean and flogging our hair with damp, salty gusts. Every few seconds the bow slaps a whitecap, spraying a curtain of mist into our weather-worn faces. Man, this would kill you if you had a weak stomach.

After traveling about 30 minutes of our two-hour passage I notice leafy mountains rising in the distant north. Then I notice, a few hundred feet to the right, our previous captain driving his single-engine boat into the wind, crouching from the spray. Then to the left a white speedboat screams past, powered by a shiny Yamaha 75 motor.

The sea roughens. The soaring bow slices through the rolling frothy monsters. Far away, on the opposite shore, a red speck pierces the grayness.

After penetrating an hour into the gulf, a plump orange sun rises from the horizon and colors the drab ocean. Meanwhile I'm watching a crab crawl along the gunwale of the boat — a boat that might be, for all we know, a smuggler's craft speeding toward Turbo with a powdery illicit cargo.

As the warm orb climbs higher over the horizon the grayness disappears and the faded red and white wood becomes a friendlier hue. But I wish I hadn't dropped my watch into the river yesterday morning. At this very moment it's probably resting on the swamp floor shrieking its alarm.

* * * *

For endless days I haven't experienced a road or a car or a hotel or a restaurant or a cold beer or an air-conditioner. But after surviving the trek through one of the planet's most punishing ecosystems, and after droning almost 24 hours through rivers and swamps and more rivers and now the sea, I'm finally approaching civilization.

To the north-northeast a leafy coast is sluggishly advancing toward us. Soon we pass it and start skirting its shoreline. I notice a Colombian military boat hugging the bank. Just beyond it the morning sun beams on a swarm of Mobil Oil tanks towering above the trees.

We follow the coastline as it curves to the left. The shoreline seems more developed. We pass a restaurant with a patio and gleaming red chairs. The speck of red I saw piercing the grayness earlier has expanded into a dirty pink boat. Then, as we pass a rusty sunken barge, I see it — my goal — the first slivers of buildings and roadways that signal Turbo, the culmination of my Darien odyssey. My heart flutters with elation as we climactically rush into the arms of the great, vast continent of South America.

The shoreline lies just a few hundred feet to portside now. I see asphalt — I see the first road that I've seen for ages. To think that I swooped onto this mighty continent by walking through such a tormenting wilderness and buzzing down a half-dozen spindly veins of water. "Am I experienced now?" I wonder to myself, after all these months, after braving the wars and the heart-wrenching poverty and the maddening injustices and the breathtaking beauty and the exhilaration and the joy and the life? Have I completed my right of passage?

We swing around another curve and leave behind the wavy sea and sprint into a harbor past a sign that warns of a 10,000-peso fine for speeding. Then we swivel around and dock against a concrete pier amidst dozens of other battered boats of every shape and size. Bordellos and saloons line the busy road. Sleazy and smelly, Turbo reinforces the image of the stereotypical Latin American port.

I hand the boat owner his 500-peso fee. Then I hoist my pack and jump over the side onto the black asphalt. I pause to examine my surroundings, especially the road — this stretch of potholed asphalt that connects down the street to the Pan-American Highway and to all the other stretches of asphalt that spiderweb through two dozen countries through mountains and fields and jungles and wastelands and span deep to the south to Tierra del Fuego on the southern tip of Chile in the near-Antarctic.

By the grace of God I survived the great rainforest. I conquered the Darien Gap.

I adjust my pack, draw a lungful of the spicy tropical air, and stroll down the bustling boulevard. My journey continues. A new continent awaits.

THE DARIEN RAINFOREST TODAY

Remarkably, this chronicle of my expedition through Darien portrayed less than half a month of my four months in Latin America.

Throughout my wandering of Central and South America I perpetually scribbled notes, filling one notebook after another. During my expedition through the magnificent rainforest, as I sweated along strenuous jungle trails and as I rushed up the frothy rivers, my shirt pocket always held a pen and a pad of paper.

After exuberantly landing in Turbo I endured hair-raising escapades in Colombia — enough to fill another book — then I journeyed to Caracas, the capital of neighboring Venezuela.

In all I rambled through nine countries in Central and South America: Mexico, Guatemala, El Salvador, Honduras, Nicaragua, Costa Rica, Panama, Colombia and Venezuela.

I never again saw or heard from the Swedes. However, one evening in cosmopolitan Cartagena on Colombia's Caribbean coast, a few weeks after my expedition ended, as I was sauntering down an elegant avenue to a sophisticated nightclub, I met the tall Dane from Unión de Choco. After we recognized each other, he related that his expedition with Paul and Walter and the Swedes had ended successfully.

And what about Prophet Mark? Well, since we were heading in the same direction, he and I traveled together for a couple of days after reaching Turbo. But by the second day he could no longer put up with what

217

he felt was my irritating chatter, especially while we were being frisked at the numerous Colombian army checkpoints, which he found harrowing and I found mundane. So we split, which was best since we're both solo travelers. I don't know what eventually happened to him, but a year after I returned home I received a postcard from Jerusalem with his signature and a message about the impending return of Christ. If anybody knows where he is today, I'd be interested to find out.

Anyway, in Caracas I phoned my mom, who works in the travel business, to ask her to help me get a ticket back home to Toronto. She offered me the choice between two flights, both about the same price — one direct to Toronto and one just across the Caribbean to Miami. I desperately wanted to get home soon, but I also wanted to crown my excursion with a challenge. "I'll take the flight to Miami," I said into the phone to my bewildered mother. "I'll hitchhike from Miami to Toronto. You should see me in a few weeks."

I actually completed the hitchhike from Miami to Toronto in about three days, after being blessed with one ride all the way from central Florida to New Jersey from a Portuguese immigrant who worked as the wine steward on a cruise ship. A few dozen hours later, on the day before my 19th birthday, I walked across the border bridge by Niagara Falls toward my Canadian home. Within a few hours I was sleeping in my parents' house in my old bedroom.

Experiencing the wars and poverty of places like Nicaragua and El Salvador transformed me. I learned to sleep with a knife under my pillow and to become a sharp character judge. I also learned to appreciate the abundant blessings showered upon us in the developed world.

Once back home I continued my studies in journalism, broadcasting and public speaking; and I soon found work writing freelance news articles. I also moved to London, England, for six months and I toured Western Europe (tame of course compared to the punishing jungle trek to Cristales). I eventually moved to Florida, opened a publishing company, worked a few stringer assignments for The Associated Press, and began writing about real estate for the local newspaper. The real estate writing eventually developed into a career as a real estate broker and a real estate investor.

As the years pass, the natives of Darien continue to inhabit their rugged, impenetrable homeland, living the way they've lived for centuries.

The wars in Central America eventually ended. Costa Rica has grown into a famous eco-tourism destination. Panama City has become one of the safer cities in Latin America.

The Darien region, however, has grown treacherous in the area near the Colombian border. Rick, the missionary from Púcuro (who worked with New Tribes Mission), was kidnapped by Colombian guerillas in 1993. Eight years later, his family found out that he had been killed after three years of captivity during a Colombian military raid on the rebels.

In 2003, Colombian paramilitary fighters attacked the Kuna native villages of Paya and Púcuro and tortured and killed several villagers. The inhabitants of both villages fled to settlements farther away from the Colombian border, to places like Boca de Cupe.

The decades-long Colombian civil war has spread to the sparsely-inhabited Katios/Darien rainforest and even forced the abandonment of the ranger station at Cristales. Fighters in the Cacarica River region around Bijao have abducted and murdered almost 100 local inhabitants over the past few years.

In 2008, the families of Rick and several other kidnapped missionaries (who are all now presumed dead) sued Chiquita Brands International Inc., alleging that the fruit company contributed to the deaths of the men because they financially supported the rebels. A few months earlier Chiquita had agreed to pay a $25 million fine for paying millions of dollars to groups in Colombia that are considered to be terrorist organizations by the United States government.

And what of the plan to bridge the gap with the Pan-American Highway? An adventurer who crossed Darien by motorcycle, American Ed Culberson, pondered whether the highway will ever be completed.

In his book OBSESSIONS DIE HARD: Motorcycling the Pan American Highway's Jungle Gap, Culberson noted that politics, finances and environmental concerns have impeded plans to connect the continents by road.

...Cuts in the federal budget, worries over the spread of Colombia's hoof-and-mouth disease and the Pan Am's perceived impact on the Indian culture had all contributed to eliminated funds...

...Without the technical and financial support of the Americans, the other [Organization of American States] members had little incentive to continue the project...Only Panama and Colombia remained dedicated to the concept — but their capabilities to carry on the work were hardly equal to the staggering task...

...the likelihood of wheeled vehicles replacing the primitive watercraft in the Darien appears to be an unreachable goal....

I completed the Darien Gap crossing when I was 18 and I finally finished writing this book in my early 20s, but it wasn't until my late 30s that I finally self-published the adventure, including updated descriptions of the Darien Rainforest today.

Of the few explorers to cross this mesmerizing jungle from the end of Panama's road to the beginning of Colombia's road, I was probably among the last, for now at least, because the war in Colombia and the violent spillover into the remote Panamanian border region made the area too dangerous for outsiders and even for the natives. By the 2010s and 2020s Panama's border police were blocking the rare cross-Darien adventurer at their new checkpoints along the jungle rivers, if they traveled too far south in Darien with plans to reach Colombia. (Occasionally an adventurer plans a journey by road, along the entire length of North and South America, from Alaska to the southern tip of Chile, by car or truck or bike or motorcycle or even on foot, only to realize that the roadless Darien

Gap will frustrate their plans. Several of them have read my book and then corresponded with me for insight about how to complete the Darien section of their adventure.)

Meanwhile, cartels began smuggling USA-bound migrants northward along Darien's rivers and trails, where many refugees would lose their possessions or even their lives.

After returning from Latin America I determined not to launch myself into any other demanding third-world excursions — I felt too burnt out.

But I soon developed the urge again. When I returned from Latin America to Toronto I couldn't even guess that exactly a year from that date I would be strolling beneath palm trees in the warm evening breeze along the West African coastline; that on that very night I would be struck by malaria; and that a few weeks afterward I would catapult into the midst of a bloody civil war where I faced tribal death squads and headless bodies amidst some of the most nefarious killing fields of the latter half of the 20th century.

I thankfully made it out with my life — barely. And as with my Latin American excursion I thoroughly detailed my African odyssey in a handful of scrappy notebooks; perhaps one day I'll publish that adventure as well.

Andrew Niall Egan
June 2008 (with revisions and edits in October 2023)

For photos, maps and other information
about this Darien expedition
or about the Darien Rainforest
visit www.AdventuraPublishing.com

Email: CrossingTheDarienGap@gmail.com